ALSO BY LAURIE NOTARO

The Idiot Girls' Action-Adventure Club

Autobiography of a Fat Bride

Autobiography of a Fat Bride

TRUE

TALES

OF

A

PRETEND

ADULTHOOD

Laurie Notaro

VILLARD

NEW YORK

Library of Congress Cataloging-in-Publication Data
Notaro, Laurie.
Autobiography of a fat bride: true tales of a pretend adulthood /
Laurie Notaro.
p.   cm.
ISBN 0-375-76092-X
1. Notaro, Laurie.   2. Humorists, American—20th century—Biography.
3. Married women—Humor.   I. Title.
PS3614.O785 Z463 2003
814'.6—dc21   2002038086

Villard Books website address: www.villard.com
Printed in the United States of America on acid-free paper
2 4 6 8 9 7 5 3
First Edition

Book design by Jo Anne Metsch

To Pop Pop,
for always making
me laugh;
and for Doug—
for then
for now
for always

Contents

Autobiography of a Fat Bride

It's Not You, It's Me

I am the sucker.

Ben's standing on the sidewalk, his hands in his pockets; his hair, normally straight and elbow-length, is now appallingly cornrowed as his head hangs toward the ground because I've caught him.

I've caught him.

He's too goddamned scared to make a move and I don't blame him, because he's my boyfriend and I caught him, just now, packing up all of his crap into a piece-of-shit hippie van because he's running off to Seattle to follow his dream, which is growing pot, smoking it, and learning to play Neil Young's "Old Man" on an acoustic guitar in order to perform it as a birthday gift for his dad, a man he has *never met*.

He is running away.

With HER.

Turn to the right, there she is, standing behind the van, trying to hide from me; it's Dog Girl, his ex-girlfriend, dressed in a tremendous gauze dress and with matching cornrow hair.

"She made the curtains," he mutters, still looking at the sidewalk.

"WHAT?" I said, shaking my head.

"She made the curtains," he repeats. "For the van. She sold her car and bought the van."

For a moment, I'm confused and I wonder about what I'm supposed to do with this. Am I supposed to fight, and kick and scream, am I supposed to oppose it? I have no idea, and I don't do anything. I just walk away.

"Don't you want to hit me?" he calls out.

"Don't you want to yell at me, tell me you hate me?" he yells to me.

I just shake my head, and keep walking.

"It's not you!" he shouts one last time. "It's me!"

That's enough to make me stop dead in my tracks.

"Really?" I ask as I spin around. "Are you *sure* it's you? Because that would make my day, just knowing that it was YOU and NOT ME, especially after I just caught you in the middle of an *escape attempt*. Is it you? Is it really you, Ben?"

"Well, I guess it's me a little bit," he stammers as Dog Girl peeks an eye out from behind the purple curtains as one of her hair ornaments chimes. "But, well, if you really want to know, I'd say that yeah, it's mostly you."

"*Mostly me?*" I reply. "It's *mostly* me that's forced you into this scene from Children of the Cornrow? God, it looks like Stevie Wonder and Bo Derek jumped you in an alley and gang-braided you!"

He stands quiet for a moment, thinking, then nods his head.

"Actually, it's pretty much all you," he adds with a sigh. "I don't think it's me at all. No, no, it's you. All you. It's not me, because the feeling that I'm getting in my chakras is that it's definitely you."

As if I needed confirmation. I've seen that play *It's Not You, It's Me* before, and as a matter of fact, I've played the lead in that scenario since before I had boobs.

My role is "Super Idiot Girl," the kind of female who searches out the most alluring sociopath to date, who never learns that if you see a tornado coming, especially one that works in a record store and displays no other ambition outside of making mixed tapes from bootleg Grateful Dead shows, duck under the nearest table until the roar passes.

It all started in fifth grade, when my mother bought me a box of valentines from Kmart. I searched out the perfect Holly Hobbie valentine, a little farmer boy in overalls milking a cow, for the boy I wanted to move into sixth grade with. Only a few days earlier, he had passed me a note, chunkily folded in the shape of a football, that said, "Whats your shampew? Gee, your hair smells terrific." It absolutely declared the love that was to guarantee me perfect happiness for the rest of my life, or at least until summer vacation. In my best cursive handwriting, I signed the back of the valentine, "To Paul, I use Breck once a week. Luv, Laurie," and, to add a sense of female intrigue, dotted the i's with puffy hearts to let him know that I was *all lady, all right.*

I can understand now how that kind of message would be chilling enough for a boy to shy away from the love of an oily-headed, prepubescent girl, but I still don't think it reached the proportions required for him to stand up during lunchtime and loudly scream, "I am NOT your boyfriend! I like Melissa Crow because she can sit on her hair and she has horses!"

When I transferred to junior high I already had a major crush on Mike Smithfield from my sixth-grade class, and had waited all summer to see him. I began parting my hair on the left out of compassion for his left-handedness, a somber physical disability that he bravely bore in a cruel right-handed world, which, at the same time, made it difficult for others to cheat off of him during tests. If I could tell that Mike Smithfield was a knight of gallantry and preeminence just by the way he faced the obstacle of the No. 2 pencil God had placed in his left hand, we were meant to be soul mates. Ideal husband material. For him, I relentlessly practiced my cutest smile, which I had noticed in a certain light was identical to the smile of the Elizabeth sister on *Eight Is Enough,* and entailed curling down the sides of my mouth and then innocently—yet strategically—pouting out my two front teeth slightly. I found it to be the perfect image of vulnerability and a girlish glow of a much-delayed, though still yet possible, sexual awakening. My mother, on the other hand, saw a premature appearance of the Elizabeth smile when she stormed into the bathroom one day and suddenly interrupted my practice time.

"Jesus Christ," she said sharply in her native Brooklyn accent, "if you had that look on your face the day I brought you home from the hospital, I probably would have laid off the cigarettes when I was pregnant with your two younger sisters. Now, I don't know what the hell you've been sniffing, but I'm telling you right now to get off smelling the paint or eating the glue or whatever, and from now on when I fill up the gas tank, you are staying in the car!!! I'll be watching for deep breaths, you know! This isn't the Linkletter house, for your information! No one in this house is getting drug crazed and then jumping off my goddamned roof! We just had that thing retarred!"

My mother had convinced herself that it was my destiny to one day simply fling myself off the roof like Art Linkletter's daughter, who vaulted to her death from the top of a six-story apartment building after taking some drugs in 1969. I'm sure it was a frightening moment for my mother, who most likely looked at me when she heard the news flash and mumbled, "Over my dead body!" despite the fact that at the time, I didn't even have the ability to chew, let alone the motor skills necessary to assemble a rig and shoot my fat little baby arm up with black-tar heroin. My "Art Linkletter's Daughter" lessons started early, when I was about nine. It happened the day my mother dropped me off for school in our Country Squire station wagon and saw a sixth-grader wearing a tie-dyed T-shirt. "See that kid?" she said, grabbing my arm and pointing to the rainbow-colored figure swinging on the monkey bars. "I bet his parents are drug people. Hippies! You know what hippies eat for dinner?"

I shook my head. "Meat on Fridays?" I ventured.

"NO!" my mother informed me. "TRASH! Hippies eat trash! They go through their neighbors' garbage and eat spoiled food because they spend all their money on drugs and art supplies!

From now on, never take a piece of gum or candy from anyone BUT ME! Never take an aspirin or drink out of the same soda can from anyone BUT ME! There are people out there, LIKE THAT HIPPIE KID, who want to get you hopped up on drugs to be like them. One day, you take a piece of gum from a girl in your PE class that makes all of the colors very bright and the world a beautiful place and the VERY NEXT DAY, you're eating rotten meat loaf out of Mrs. Kelch's trash bin and you're not wearing underwear. That's a loose life! Art Linkletter's daughter jumped off the roof after someone gave her some gum, and although nobody says it, I bet she ate trash, too. Is that the kind of life you want to lead? A loose life? IS IT?"

I spent a long time believing that a sabotaged stick of funky Juicy Fruit, a Mr. Pibb laced with a Bayer aspirin, or an angel dust–spiked Jolly Rancher would fill me with pulsating, uncontrollable urges to locate my father's ladder, scramble up it, and then fling myself off our one-story spec house like a virgin sacrifice and then flatten my mother's yucca plant like a lily pad. Honestly, in hindsight, I don't think it was the possibility of my experiencing a drug-related death that scared my mother as much as the possibility of her being known as "Mrs. Notaro, who's addict daughter jumped off the roof" that sunk a worry knife in her straight to the bone. However, since I believed that most of the people in my environment were trying to get me to fly off a roof (that is, until I was twenty-five and finally understood that no one gives away free drugs to people they don't know because friends always come first), I was faced with an undeniable love dilemma when I saw Mike Smithfield on the first day of middle school.

I spotted him poised at the trash can in the cafeteria, his tray held gingerly with his left hand, and I rushed over to say hi. He nodded, smiled slightly, and I gawked.

A tense, long moment passed before he said suddenly, "Um, want this Snoball?" and pointed to the pink, coconut-flecked mound that teetered on the edge of the tray, a mere millisecond away from mating with a cold, mottled Salisbury-steak patty that waited eagerly in the trash heap below. A four-star hippie dinner, I remembered thinking.

Understanding the potential of a poisoned bakery product, I was naturally wary, though the spongy, marshmallowy goodness and the fluffy-filling creaminess called out to my spiking hormones in nothing less than a siren song. No, Mike Smithfield was not my mother. That was true. But he *was* a lefty. An underdog. A social cripple. He understood pain, he knew it well. Those who weep are the last ones to cause a tear. I believed I could trust him. Besides, if he needed me to jump off a roof to prove my love, I would soar like an ostrich.

I nodded back and slowly looked up as I launched the Elizabeth smile, poked out my two donkey teeth, and plucked up the Snoball with my *left* hand. Knowing that this Snoball gift was a sure sign of tender affection, and given the fact the I was wearing my new, cute pair of brick-red Dittoes, I sucked up all of my courage in one deep breath and said, "Wanna go with me to the Sadie Hawkins dance on Friday?"

"No," he said simply, but I didn't believe him. I knew better. Boys will be shy. They are afraid of love, I told myself, you must coax them, show them the love light. I followed him all the way to his PE class at the gym with the Elizabeth smile frozen on my face as I asked, "Why? Why won't you go with me? Why?" until we hit the baseball field and he just took off running. He ran the entire length of the field, constantly looking over his shoulder to see if I was still chasing him. I stood there for a long time, understanding slowly that Snoballs, although pink and soft, didn't always mean love. At that precise moment, Patti Herman, the first girl who smoked at our school and the one most likely to force you to eat a hallucinogenic stick of Big Red in the girls' bathroom, walked by me and said, "Hey! Do you think your pants are tight enough, Cameltoe? You don't even need to wear pants if you're going to show off your cookie like that!"

Things weren't about to get better, even after that.

My romantic life took a violent turn my sophomore year in high school. I was adoringly watching Jim Kroeger, a senior, play basketball in the gym when he called my name for the first time. I turned around and flashed my biggest, brightest, newly practiced Chrissy Snow bucktoothed smile just in time for him to bounce the basketball right off my head. I got up, dazed but still smiling amid the laughter rolling in waves around me, and smiled all the way to the nurse, who looked at the round, patterned welt on my forehead and asked me if I had seizures often.

Later in high school, I dated an older, nearly high school graduate from Los Angeles whom I worked with at a Pizza D'Amore (The Pizza of Love) in the mall. With romance sparking between every dough ball and sprinkle of mozzarella, our eyes met, except the one he had that was a little bit lazy. When he pulled in front of my house that night in a green Chevy van with the windows painted black, my mother chased him away, waving a dish towel and screaming, "Put it in reverse and back it up, buddy! You're not getting your greasy pizza paws on my kid, Mr. California!"

In college, I had enough experience that I should have taken note of the red flag when it popped up on dates, especially on the ones when the guy was already drunk when I went to pick him up. It was always a bad sign, because I figured if I had the foresight to remain sober for the most promising portion of the date, the guy should have the same kind of hope, too. One such potential mate, now referred to by friends as "The Horror of Todd," was a guy that I met in a communications law class who was not only drunk when I went to pick him up, he was *unconscious*. After my pounding at the front door woke him up, he accompanied me to dinner and proceeded to eat an entire cheeseburger without the use of his hands. He would look up every now and then, his face smeared with ketchup, meat flecks, and chewed-up bits of lettuce, and simply whine at me like a hyena at a carcass.

I, on the other hand, was determined to work things out. I tried as hard as I could to pretend that everything was fine, saying things like "So, how long did it take you to make the rainbow—oh, I'm sorry, *light prism*—in your living room out of beer bottles?" "I think it's fascinating that you can play every Dave Matthews song by blowing into a beer bottle," "It takes a certain kind of talent to make a wind chime out of a beer bottle," and "No, Todd, I really don't think that will fit up your nose, being that it's a *beer bottle*."

I began dating another guy I met at a bar until I found him engaged in a random sex act with a teenaged dairy queen, her little red apron crumpled up at the foot of the couch, but that was really okay because I was looking for a way out ever since I found a Special Olympics medal in his room. It gave me the opportunity to return his gift of the Lego block version of the Millennium Falcon that I thought was so wacky and displayed a madcap sense of humor instead of his current stage of mental development. I finally understood that he just may not have had a serious drinking problem after all, and figured it might be a wise idea to call a lawyer and prepare for my courtroom defense. My boyfriend after that planted his seed in a uterus that wasn't mine, and I eventually got over it by losing thirty pounds and dating his best friend, who then realized girls really grossed him out.

So I graduated from college with a degree in journalism and was ready to find my dream job at a newspaper in addition to one good man who owned his own car and was certain about his sexuality, my two new, revised qualifying criteria for a potential date.

I had the exceptional bad fortune to enter the job market at the same time the morning daily newspaper bought out the afternoon daily newspaper, merged the two, and 250 reporters and editors found themselves without employment. Though I successfully scored an interview at another small paper as an obituary writer, I eventually lost out to a former features editor with twenty years' experience.

So I began my life as Brenda Starr, cub receptionist for a small music distributor. My friend Kate worked there in the accounting department, and mentioned that the last receptionist had been let go after she was found naked at her desk, talking to clients who didn't actually exist. It was an easy job. I didn't have to dress up, just *remain* dressed, and I was hired on the spot after I reassured the general manager that I had never heard or, most important, answered to voices that called out to me from beyond demanding that I disrobe. The job had two perks: a 25 percent employee discount on records and the option that I didn't have to wear my Wonderbra if I didn't want to. In fact, it was encouraged that I leave it in a drawer at home.

There were plenty of handsome boys working in the warehouse, but I figured it would be wise not to shit where I ate. Besides, the handsomest one—this guy with alluringly sensitive eyes—would barely speak to me, even though I tried desperately to impress him with my knowledge and expertise at the copy machine. I was a college graduate, after all. He had a warm smile and those incredible eyes that avoided all contact with mine, almost like I was a tick that was trying to suck out his soul with my womanly stare. I tried to break the ice one day when one of his copies jammed, so I immediately jumped up to perform surgery on the machine, successfully freeing the renegade sheet of paper. I showed him the culprit and closed up the innards, but his response was slightly less than the magnificent awe I was expecting. He looked at me for only a moment, grabbed the paper from my hand, and then fled back into the warehouse.

Kate laughed when I recounted the story later that day, and I was horrified when she pointed out a little tiny booger in my left nostril that poked its milky, wormy head out every time I exhaled. Then we met up for happy hour, and Kate bought me a drink after work, and we toasted the fact that mucus was a beautiful preventative measure to shitting where you were about to take a big bite.

Super Idiot Girl: The Sad Life and Lonely Times of Princess Enabler

Ben had fled the state like I was the Khmer Rouge. I had, however, been warned.

On our first date, he stood me up.

"I just couldn't make it. I couldn't get a ride" was Ben's excuse, because, naturally, he didn't have a car.

Our second date took place in a park because we were apparently hiding from his girlfriend, her existence of which, at this point, I was unaware; the third date took place behind the counter of the record store (more hiding) in which he worked, as we ate Whoppers with cheese we got on a two-for-one deal. We shared french fries and a drink, and also note that these were not supersized. You would think that I would be catching on by now, but I'm still blissfully unaware—I'm mesmerized by his goatee.

I am a stoopid girl, and the kind of stoopid you spell with two o's.

The entire duration of our liaison lasted the lifetime of one hurricane season, and created enough damage to qualify as a state of emergency. In the span of a week, our status quickly jumped from a date in the park to my designation as his "own lovely lady."

Never a good sign.

As it turns out, Ben had a pretty big character flaw.

We were on our way to a party one night when Ben mentioned his unstable girlfriend. I was getting ready to dive into my "The Injury I Incurred By Walking Into A Steel Light Pole During A Third-Grade Field Trip Simply Made Me More Sensitive As A Person, Which Is Quite Different From Unstable, I'll Have You Know" speech until I realized he wasn't talking about me.

Beware the Girlfriend: It's always a weary tale, and usually pops up in Act Three of "It's Not You, It's Me," so Ben's ex-girlfriend made a cameo rather early. Preexisting girlfriends are always a rickety lot; they're never biochemists, financial wizards, or English professors. They're almost always on some sort of behavior-modifying medication, or probation. The ones I've had the misfortune to tangle with have usually not finished high school, let alone had careers. Ben's girlfriend got the closest to having a career, due to her job as a trimmer at a dog grooming business.

"What do you mean, there's a 'girlfriend'?" I asked him as we arrived at our destination. "You're not allowed more than one, because I know you're not a Mormon and you're not a sheikh. You don't even have a car, let alone the funds to provide for a *harem*. You can't get Whoppers on a three for one deal, you know!"

Ben stumbled into the explanation that they weren't really *together* together; things had fizzled out, but they were still living in the same apartment because neither could afford to move.

Honestly, it didn't sound all that weird to me, since my friend Jamie had lived uncomfortably under that arrangement for an entire six months until she came home one day and found that her ex-boyfriend, now roommate, had donated most of her possessions to charity when he found out she was dating again.

Ben then quickly offered proof that they were no longer *together* together.

"You can call me at the apartment anytime," he said confidently as we knocked on the door. "It's okay with her. I told her about you."

That was good proof, I thought, pretty rock solid, even though I reasoned that if my ex-boyfriend's new girlfriend called my house, I'd probably hang right up and call Goodwill, too.

Dog Girl must be very understanding, I thought, as I walked

into the party, still unable to grasp the whole concept. But in about ten seconds, I was even further stunned when Ben broke into a rather mortifying interpretive dance to George Clinton and Parliament's "Tear the Roof Off the Sucker" after taking a hit off what could be called a questionable cigarette. While I shrank into a corner, he pranced around the living room like a Budweiser Clydesdale, shimmied like Gypsy Rose Lee, and then ate an entire bowl of French onion dip with his index finger.

It was exactly one week later that I found Ben and Dog Girl packing up his stuff into her hippie van, and he told me it was all my fault. I could only think of one thing to say as I walked back to my car.

"Oh, yeah?" I yelled. "Well, you two TRASH EATERS deserve each other since I know HE couldn't pick out a fork in a lineup!!!"

It's better this way, I kept repeating inside my head as I got in the car and put the gear in drive, leaving them both on the curb, standing next to the van. It's better this way.

What kind of man dates a Cornrow Girl? I ask myself.

What kind of woman gets dumped for a Cornrow Girl?

I picture my scalp partitioned, sectioned, and woven like a Shaker basket, and I shiver.

My boyfriend just ran away, I thought. To another state. With Medusa.

Maybe he just took some bad drugs.

Bad drugs will totally make a person do things like that; look what he did after one hit off a joint, he morphed into David Lee Roth! Besides, my cousin once killed a cat when he was on acid and burglarizing a house, because he thought it was a lion.

Bad drugs can cause a boyfriend to desert you.

Be realistic, I reminded myself. No amount of drugs, good or bad, could have made those cornrows into anything but cornrows. A cat can be a lion, but a cornrow is still *bad hair*.

It really is my fault, I tell myself. I need to learn to recognize and identify the danger signs when I see them, and not brush them off as "eccentricities," "lovable oddities," or "a sign that he is crying out for the help and the comforting of a codependent nurturer that only I, Princess Enabler, can provide." Bad boyfriends don't disguise themselves; their girlfriends do it for them. I was guilty of that. A bad boyfriend will stay as such, and rarely, rarely, will a good boyfriend wake up one day and defect to the evil forces. By the same token, a bad boyfriend will never, ever wake up one day and become a good one. You've got a better chance of finding a dead rat in a soda can and becoming a millionaire in the settlement afterward. A bad boyfriend will not change, because, simply, there's no shame in it for him.

But there should be consequences, there should be penalties: he lies, and I get to witness the tattooing of the words "Warning: Severe Emotional Danger Ahead: Use of this product may cause temporary blindness, hysteria, irrationality, low self-esteem, and could require psychiatric care of a trained professional at the rate of $120 an hour plus a $15 copay," preferably on his forehead.

I was the sucker.

I am the sucker.

So I did the only thing I could. Before the sun even had a chance to rise, I was on a plane to Portland, Oregon, where my runner-up boyfriend was waiting for me at the gate. Our newfound bliss lasted approximately thirty minutes, until we pulled into his driveway and he said simply, "Just so you know, my ex-girlfriend moved back in because cash was real tight, man. But don't worry, don't freak out, okay, 'cause it's totally cool. I told her all about you."

You Never Call Me

After discovering that my backup boyfriend's roommate was not merely a former girlfriend but a size-six, raven-haired beauty with not one, single freckle and a flawless complexion, I decided to cut my stay short by a couple of days. When I realized that she was from FRANCE, pronounced my name "Loh-wee!" and got regularly manicured, I folded my hand and hopped on the next flight home. I had already lost out to a dog girl; there was no way I was going head-to-head with a skinny little Frenchie with perfect nails and healthy skin who could eat troughs of cheese without the ramifications.

Several weeks after my aborted runaway attempt, I was tearing apart my purse for the hint of a cigarette when I found the phone number. Caught in the clutches of a nicotine fit, I held the torn piece of paper with shaking hands and wondered aloud how I had gotten it.

"Thanks for fixing the paper jam, you never call me. 967-8564."

I looked at the number for a while, and then suddenly, I gasped.

The guy from work, the warehouse guy, the guy who saw the wormy booger pop out of my nose! The sensitive eyes guy! Oh my God.

Wait—

Oh my God.

Slowly, pieces of a previous blackout start floating by, like I'm catching glimpses of a dream.

Oh, I *hate* it when this happens! Now I have to figure out if Sensitive Eyes guy saw me naked!

MEMORY: A week earlier, I'm at Long Wong's, my favorite bar. There's laughing, I remember laughing, that's always good, laughing is good. Okay, I'm holding a drink in a lowball, it's a full drink, Sensitive Eyes guy is laughing at something I said. Or maybe a particle of my brain just tumbled out of my nostril, I don't know. He comes a little closer, and I think he said, "You're so pretty"— that can't be right—but I'm not so sure because then the full drink slips out of my hand and dives toward the floor, where it shatters into a million little diamonds.

Oh boy. Too drunk to hold on to a whiskey and Coke and the word "pretty." That's not a combination with a positive outcome. Not good at all. That's the secret password that usually leaves me trying to find a ride home in the morning. If Sensitive Eyes Guy didn't see me naked, it's a strong bet that I at least flashed him a boob, and if I did, I certainly hope it was the bigger—and firmer—of the two.

That's it. I'm going to have to quit my job. Or call him. If he saw me naked, I'll have to quit anyway.

So I dialed the number on the mangled piece of paper, I called Sensitive Eyes Guy, and, lo and behold, a *lady* answered.

A LADY. Like a MOM lady. Or, with my luck, a wife.

I was so caught off guard that I actually left a message instead of my usual MO of hanging up. And the funny thing was that when the phone rang in an hour, I thought it was him calling back, most likely to tell me that after our conjugal visit he was experiencing some pronounced sensations that may require the care of a medical professional.

It wasn't.

Instead, it was my good friend Troy, who I had worked with on the college newspaper. He said that some guy gave him three thousand dollars to start a magazine and did I want a job as a music editor? The pay was shitty, there were no benefits, but we could smoke in the office, which was upstairs from a guy who made pornos, and sell the promo CDs we got for drinking money. Did that sound cool?

"Cooler than Keith Richards when you could still understand what he was saying," I said. "I can start immediately."

I called a girl I knew who was looking for a job, and I was sure she'd be perfect for my old one at the music distributor. Since I also knew that the work-history portion of her application would list past employers such as Babe's Cabaret, Sally's Strutters, and Starlite Lounge and All-Nude Review, the issue of leaving her bra at home was entirely nonexistent.

And then I happily forgot about Sensitive Eyes Guy and the fact that he never called me back. Especially since *he lived with his mom.* Well, that's a lie. I mean, it's true, I dated the retarded guy from the Special Olympics, I dated the Horror of Todd, I dated a hippie, I dated a man who's homosexuality I had vigorously awakened, but none of those guys was holed up with his mom. Okay, one guy I dated lived in a halfway house, which could kind of be considered the same thing, but honestly, I just thought he had a roommate with some aggression/control issues who preferred "lights out" at a certain time. Plus the fact that I'd much rather deal with a parole officer than *a mom,* I'd rather deal with a SWAT team than *a mom.* And he didn't even have the guts to call me back!

And that's exactly what I was planning on telling Mr. My-Eyes-Are-Not-Nearly-As-Sensitive-As-They-May-Appear-Guy the next time I saw him at Long Wong's. I was planning on giving him a Hungry Man helping of "what for," hopefully when I had a couple of drinks under my belt, *which was staying ON this time.* I had my chance several months later when I walked into the bar and there he was, drinking a beer with a friend of his.

I was just about to ask him what time his mother was going to pick him up or if she was already waiting in the parking lot with the engine of her station wagon running when he turned around and waved when he saw me.

"Hey," he said cheerfully. "How have you been? I heard you got a new job."

"Yeah," I answered weakly, disarmed by his niceness and those horribly consistent sensitive eyes. "How is my replacement working out?"

"Great. She showed up for the interview three hours late wearing roller skates and a tube top," he answered. "They hired her on the spot."

"That's fabulous," I said, trying to get the bartender's attention.

"You," Mr. You-Cannot-Ignore-The-Hypnotizing-Power-Of-My-Sensitive-Eyes said, "never call me."

"Okay," I said, turning around sharply as I slapped my hand loudly on the bar. "Let's put that line to bed, shall we? I mean, I don't know how many girls you get to call your house and talk to your mom or wife or whatever she is with that ploy, but I'm not going to fall for it again. You know, most felons that I've dated are more straightforward than you. We had one night of drunken, most likely backseat gymnastics and I'm perfectly happy to leave it at that."

He looked at me like I had an eel-size booger inching out of my nostril this time.

"Oh my God," he said, shocked. "You're Gloria!"

"You're an asshole," I nearly yelled. "But for the record, I'm LAURIE, although I'm hoping Gloria has a rack as firm as a Sealy Posturepedic Mattress."

"No, I mean, you're *Gloria*," he said excitedly. "You're the girl who called! My mom gave me a message that a 'Gloria' called me, but I don't know anyone named Gloria and it's been driving me crazy trying to figure it out. But I just did! Laurie! Gloria! You're *Gloria!*"

Really, I didn't know whether to believe him or not. I've bought

much flimsier lines, for example, "I live with my EX-girlfriend."
But he seemed sincere, he seemed like he was telling the truth.

And after all, I *was* the sucker.

"Okay, fine," I said, giving in. "You win, I believe you. Maybe. I
think. I don't know. And although I probably don't want to know
this, what happened that night I saw you here? How well do you
know . . . *Gloria*? In the biblical sense?"

"What do you mean?" he said, looking puzzled.

I sighed. "What I mean is, did you just see the Sealy Posturepedic Mattress in the showroom," I tried to explain, "or did you
take it for a test lay, so to speak?"

"Oh," he answered, nodding his head. "Oh. You mean coitus.
Did we mate, that's what you mean. You want to know if there was
copulation."

"Yes," I answered. "It would be nice to know so I could make an
informed decision if I should run out of here like I was on fire,
suddenly blurt out, 'Sometimes I wear underpants made out of
fake black monkey fur,' or if the one shred of dignity I now have
left is stuck in my teeth like I just ate a chimichanga."

He took a deep breath. "No," he said. "Your virtue was valiantly
defended by a plummeting lowball full of JD and Coke that landed
on my foot and fractured my pinky toe. Frankly, I was in far too
much pain to think you were still cute or even vaguely attractive at
that point. Agony will do that to any man."

"Wow," I said, "I'm really sorry. I had no idea I harmed you first."

"Well, you know," he replied with a smirk, "you were rather
busy the moment after you shattered several of my bones. I mean,
you kind of get distracted when two bouncers take it upon themselves to physically remove you from the premises."

"That explains the marks around the wrists." I tried to laugh.
"See, I thought you told me I was smart, too."

He smiled. "You are pretty and you are smart," he mentioned.
"And I would like to hang out with you. But please hold your drink
at least two feet away from me. I'm just starting to get feeling back
in my foot."

"You keep talking like that and a foot isn't the only thing that's going to get broken around here," I said, knowing full well that if I had even remotely learned from past lessons, that if I had picked up even one slim thread of knowledge as a result of my poor decision-making skills and a flagrantly out-of-control id, that if I didn't run away as if he had just said, "Oh, those were monkey underpants? Whew! I thought it was just the Italian in you coming out to meet me," then it was all in vain. All of it. Watching Ben, his Dog Girl, and my stereo squeal away in a van; witnessing the Horror of Todd bury his face in a burger basket and emerge with a curly fry wedged into his nostril; looking at My Left-Handed Love tear across a baseball field as if he had seen an incubated reptilian gargoyle burst out of my chest cavity when actually it was the Snoball inside me crying; finding out that to my runner-up Portland boyfriend I was only the runner-up girlfriend—it was all in vain.

And I was still the sucker.

"If you have ever competed in the Special Olympics or another woman is carrying your progeny at this moment, the deal's off," I said slowly and cautiously. "And lift up your pant leg; I know the difference between a diabetic ID bracelet and an electronic monitoring cuff, you know, so don't even try it."

"All clear," he assured me.

"And if your mom always gets the top bunk, this is so over," I informed him.

"We've been fighting over that a lot less since my landlord fixed the air-conditioning in my apartment," he said.

"Let's get one thing straight then," I said as I looked him dead in his sensitive eyes. "It's not me, it's you, got it? It's YOU, it's not ME. It's *never* going to be me. IT will always be YOU. Got it?"

"So it's not you, it's me?" he said.

"Right," I said.

The Good Guy

I had wanted a good boyfriend all of my life, and when I finally got one, I had no idea what to do with him.

He called when he said he would.

He held my hand when other people were watching.

He had his own car, which, coincidentally, *actually ran*.

His ex-girlfriend lived in another state and although she was currently pregnant, it was BY ANOTHER MAN, and a demonstrated pie chart/time line proved that my boyfriend's chromosomes could not have, in any way, been detected in a DNA paternity test.

One night, after an evening of drinking, he told me he loved me in a Denny's parking lot at 2 A.M., and then he bought me a Grand Slam breakfast. When he sobered up the next day, he didn't even take what he said back or ask me to pay half of the check.

What do you do with a guy like that?

I had no idea. I have to admit I was completely perplexed.

All I could do was keep waiting for the Real Boyfriend in him to come out, because I knew the craven creature had to be in there *somewhere*, lurking. I mean, it's *inborn*. This one, I figured, was the most patient and affectionate sociopath I had ever dated. One night as he slept, I hovered over the breathing patterns of my boyfriend and whispered, "I command thy demon to show himself!" but all that happened was that the poor little fellow started to drool.

I tried to ask my friends for advice, but they all looked at me as if I were crazy.

"What do you mean he's never made you cry?" my friend Nikki said. "How else are you supposed to know he likes you!"

"Are you serious that he's never stood you up?" my friend Sara said. "That sounds a little . . . *clingy* if you ask me."

"I can't believe he hasn't asked you for a loan yet," my friend Kate said. "He must have another girlfriend with a better job."

"I agree, it's highly unusual," my best friend Jamie mentioned, scratching her chin. "But could it be—Nah. No. Nope. No way. I mean, I don't think so, what are the chances? Are you really, completely sure that he's not working undercover, perhaps as a religious missionary attempting to save your damned soul or a guy who's trying to sell you life insurance or a mutual fund?"

"I'm pretty sure," I disclosed.

"You know, I've heard there was one out there, one left, running and living among them." She nodded. "I always took it as a tall tale, an urban legend, an archetype of mythical proportions, but maybe he is out there. I believe there were several strands of hair discovered on a bush one time, as well as a questionable poop. Apparently, he's been spotted, according to several notable anthropologists, but never identified. Based on what I've heard, from his appearance, he's indistinguishable from the rest."

"The rest of *who*?" I asked.

"Men," she said simply. "The rest of men. I don't want to freak you out, but I think you've found him."

"Found *who*?" I asked.

She smiled. "The Good Guy," she said with a wink.

I freaked out. I mean, this was *pressure*. If he really was a Good Guy, the weight on my shoulders was insurmountable. Because that meant I had to keep him; if I spooked him or chased him away or introduced him to any of my attractive friends, I would never find another of his kind. Therefore I was facing incredible challenges.

He was an endangered species; the only thing that could make him more valuable was if he were albino. If I had any chance of keeping the Good Guy, I was going to have to start wearing clean clothes. Stop eating sugar and let my face clear up. I was probably going to have to cook. I was definitely going to have to shave. It looked like I might have to *compromise* on occasion.

Honestly, there was no chance that a girl like me, with all of her scratches and her dents, was going to be able to hang on to a guy like that, not even if I grew hawklike talons—it might take my nails up to a week to reach their full, puncture-level maturity. I was not a shiny, gleaming, firm Red Delicious or a fuzzy, blushing Georgia peach. My fruit was bruised and came with its own colony of Med flies.

I embarked on the only option open to me, considering the limitations of my talents and skills. Plan A involved taking him to the bar and plying him with alcohol, keeping the man as inebriated and befuddled for as long as humanly possible. By the time he sobered up, it would be time to send him off to work, where he would be too consumed with dehydration and alcohol poisoning to realize there was a gap between my two front teeth. Or that they were slightly bucked, given the four years of relentless lying on my behalf when documenting the usage on my headgear chart. Or that they were the color of butter. Or that I had a mole under my lip, which by the time I reached middle age would be mistaken for an M&M, and by the time I had gone gray and my ass was slapping the back of my knees when I walked would effloresce into the size of a giant gumdrop, undoubtedly knocking my nose into second place in the pecking order for the largest feature of my face.

Oh yeah. I had problems, all right, and they were about to get worse.

He mentioned that he wanted me to meet his family over the Christmas holiday, and that was when I felt the possibility of the love balloon deflate. What was I going to do then? How could I possibly intoxicate all of his kin, including the children? Nyquil would probably work for any of them in the featherweight category, but for the full-size adults, I'd have to inject commercial-grade heroin into the Butterball. My cover would be blown, and I would be revealed for the day-old fruit that I was. Besides, I didn't want to meet his family so soon—we had only been dating for a couple of months, and frankly, that's not even enough time for a primate to bond with its mother, let alone try to get the Catch of the Century attached to me. I had visions of myself walking through the door and meeting his mother for the first time, as she looked at me as if she had just seen me slide down a brass pole wearing nothing but a string of fake pearls.

So I was forced to stop getting my boyfriend drunk, which was probably a good thing, I figured, since sobriety may have given him the opportunity to learn my last name. I started trying to prepare myself for the family introduction, telling myself, "How bad could it be? There's bound to be an introduction in the history of the world that had more horrific consequences; President Clinton and Monica Lewinsky, Angelo Buono and Kenneth Bianchi, Elton John and Bernie Taupin. Rush Limbaugh and a microphone." I had miles to go before I reached that level of disaster, and the time had come to call in my reinforcement talents now that I could no longer turn my boyfriend into a blithering alcoholic. Aside from getting a bartender's attention quickly and ordering drinks at the bar, I only had one talent left: frying cutlets.

Certainly, in some areas of the world, frying cutlets is a menial task, but in the land of the Italian-American-Catholic hierarchy, cutlet frying could easily take the place of beauty and could even forgive a sin as ugly as infertility, especially in a marriage-aged woman with an above-average number of moles. Now, in this specific culture, frying a perfect cutlet, comparatively speaking, is equal to the ability of a woman of Germanic stock to plow a field by herself without even assistance from livestock, of an English-woman for keeping most of her teeth a variation of the color "pale," or the duty of a Mormon woman to pop out a baby every birthing season for a decade straight without missing even one year.

And it just so happens, I can fry a mean cutlet.

I'm sure it's no mistake, either. I'm nearly positive that when I was five and the baby freckle under my lip began to assert itself as a growth, my mother gasped, "Jesus, Mary, and Joseph, when the time comes to marry her off, that thing will be the size of a brown Volkswagen. Egg, bread crumbs, frying pan, Laurie! Egg, bread crumbs, frying pan, pay attention!" If there had been a fry-off, I would have won it hands down before I even realized this was my only chance at love, but due to the fact that my parents had up-rooted my sisters and me from our native Brooklyn to the desolate shit hole known as Phoenix, Arizona, my title as the Cutlet Queen tragically went uncrowned. There was no way my gift could be appreciated, let alone recognized in a land that called a dinner roll a "bagel." In hindsight, our neighbors were nice to us simply because they were afraid my Italian New Yorker father would, at any minute, start shaking down the block for protection money or insist on selling them fur coats in 118-degree weather that he said fell off a truck (though in Arizona, you'd say "fell offer this here waggin"). After all, they believed we must have been related to the Gambino crime family because our last names ended with the very same letter. Arizona was new territory to New York Italians, evidenced when, on our first day in our new desert home, the unafraid and impeccably tanned leader of the Welcome Wagon ladies brought over a pan of lasagna made of cottage cheese, Ragu, and Velveeta. My mother promptly responded by running out to the front yard, waving her arms and screaming, trying frantically to flag down the disappearing Mayflower moving truck as it turned the corner and was gone forever.

But it was now apparent to me that my cutlet prowess had not been in vain; now was my time to shine in order to keep my boyfriend hooked. I pounded, I floured, I dipped. I fried. And I fried. And I fried. Veal cutlets. Beef cutlets. Chicken cutlets. If I could hit it with a hammer and it stayed still long enough for me to submerge it in an egg wash then bathe it in bread crumbs, it became a cutlet. Soon, I didn't own a single piece of clothing that didn't bear the scars of an exploding oil bubble, my skin was covered with tiny red oil burns that looked disturbingly like the pox, and everything I owned became laminated with a thin, grimy sheen.

And my poor boyfriend, who had been raised on a steady diet of pressed meats and Dinty Moore stew, didn't have the first inclination of how to handle it.

"Wow, I never knew you could do this," he said the first time I placed a pan of chicken Parmesan in front of him, as he looked at me with a smile that said he thought I was a goddess. "I didn't know you could cook! You can cook! You never told me you could cook! I haven't had a home-cooked meal since the last time my mom made . . . *toast* . . . for our chopped ham sandwiches! This is incredible! Wow! You can cook!"

And then he gobbled the whole pan of chicken Parmesan down like he was a hominid who didn't know if he would survive long enough for a next meal. It was simply beautiful. I had laid the cutlet trap, and the Good Guy had fallen headfirst into it.

When I felt that I had securely gotten him hooked on cutlets, that he was now a junkie with a hunger that no other woman could fix or satisfy, I stood above him as he ravaged a casserole dish of veal piccata.

"Look at this!" I yelled, pointing to my lip. "Look at this mole! Some day, especially if I'm exposed to enough radiation, this thing will be mammoth enough in size to require its own pillow at night! Do you understand that?"

"That's a mole?" he said, barely looking up. "I thought that was just a permanent smudge because you eat so much chocolate. I'm glad to know it's not a food particle, that's a relief!"

Then he wolfed down another piece of veal as a caper rolled from his chin.

I had dared the demon to show itself, and it had.

It just turned out that it was me.

Dog Girl Bites Back

When the phone rang, the last person I expected to hear on the other end was Dog Girl.

It had been months since I found both of them, my boyfriend and his newly reinstated girlfriend, packing up his stuff into her VW van right before they planned to flee the state as if they had been profiled on *America's Most Wanted* the night before.

"I know it's weird that I'm calling," Dog Girl said nervously.

I didn't know what to say, so I offered the first comment that volunteered itself. "Do you still have my stereo?" I asked.

"No," she answered. "We sold it and bought beads and hemp cord so we could start a hair-beading booth on the Renaissance-fair circuit."

"Oh, that's right," I mentioned. "I forgot how good you were at braiding hair. What do you want, what can I help you with? Why are you calling me?"

"Well, I—I—I have bad news," Dog Girl sputtered. "I have GONORRHEA!"

I just held the phone, shocked.

"And so do you!" she added, then broke down into sobs.

I didn't know what to say. All I knew at that moment was that I wished my skin would slink off my body the way it does on a boiled tomato.

"What are you talking about?" I finally shot out as Dog Girl wept hysterically.

"At A Royal Afayre in Sacramento, Ben said that he was burning a bit, but he thought he just took some bad peyote or something," she said, in between gulps and gasps. "And by the time we were setting up for Gates of Thyme Faire the next weekend, he said he was on fire. He smoked a whole quarter ounce and he was still crying so hard I had to help him to the first aid station. He just kept saying, 'Ow ow ow ow ow! It hurts, it hurts, it hurts!' the very same thing he said when Jerry Garcia left us for the next plane of reality."

"Wow, the first aid station, huh? A regular trip to the hippie hospital," I replied. "Can you skip to my link in the venereal disease chain, please?"

"Well, the nurse looked at him and said that it was probably gonorrhea," Dog Girl answered. "And that's when he mentioned your name."

"Oh, I see," I said rather dryly. "He didn't care enough to say good-bye before I found the two of you leaving on the midnight train to Georgia, but I'm supposed to believe he has enough compassion to ask you to call me as a courtesy?"

"Well, in a way, I guess," she continued. "Since he said he got his burning penis from you."

If I had had enough money to buy a new phone, I would have thrown that one into the wall. If I had had enough money to build a new wall, I would have thrown that phone very hard. If I had had medical insurance, even with an HMO, I would have put my fist through the wall right after I threw the phone, even though the HMO would have only paid for three of my five broken fingers.

"How could I have given *him* VD?" I instead raged into the phone. "I went to college! I have a car! I'm not the one that cheats! And I can't name *one* Grateful Dead song besides 'Truckin' '!"

"Well, that's what he said," Dog Girl said limply.

"Put him and his flaming genitals on the phone," I growled. "*Right now!*"

"I can't!" Dog Girl said as she started to cry again. "He ran off with someone else, and I'm pretty sure it was Lady Jane, because her face-painting booth hasn't been set up all day! Why would he leave me like that, and take all of the penicillin, too? I can't believe it! We were even talking about getting our own Kettle Korn cart to hook up to the van!"

"Wow, that's even a broader horizon than his previous life goal of growing his own pot," I added. "Well, aside from learning 'Old Man' on a five-string so he could sing it to a stranger that might be his dad."

I realized that this was really starting to sound like the Leif Garrett episode of Behind the Music.

"I guess I should have known something was fishy when Lady Jane showed up at the van with a guitar one night and started singing that same, exact song. It always makes Ben cry, especially the 'twenty-four and so much more' part," Dog Girl recalled sadly.

"I have to go," I said quickly. "I think I'd better call the clinic before word gets out in this part of the country that Ben has VD. Once that happens, I might not be able to get an appointment for months. Renaissance fairs all up and down the West Coast will empty out and head for Planned Parenthood. But I suppose they can call it 'Plague Day.'"

After I hung up, I sat on the edge of my bed for a long time, until I had smoked almost a pack of cigarettes, until it got dark, until my new, hopelessly perfect, wonderfully wonderful boyfriend came over.

"Hi!" he said as he flipped on the light and exposed his sexually transmitted disease–ridden girlfriend. "I'm starving! What kind of cutlets are we having tonight?"

"I'm not cooking," I said, staring at the floor. "I'm breaking up with you. I'm sorry."

"What?" my boyfriend said hoarsely.

"It's not you," I heard myself say. "It's me. It really, truly is me."

"I'm not getting this," he said as I kept my eyes on the floor.

"You don't have to, because I'm doing you a favor," I told him, finally looking at his bewildered face. "I should only be the Backup Girlfriend. You deserve someone better than the backup for your first string. I can unjam a Xerox machine, I can get a drink in seconds flat, and I can fry cutlets. That's it. That's all I've got."

"You have way more than that," he said, sitting down next to me on the bed. "Those are silly things. You have so much more than those things."

"Actually, you're right," I agreed. "Because apparently, I have the clap, too. Or I *may* have the clap. Which means I might have graciously passed it on to you, brought to you by the Ghost of Boyfriends Past. Dog Girl called today to pass on the news of what Ben passed on to her, and maybe me. I'm sorry, I'm beyond sorry."

"Wow, that's not good news," he said after a moment, and then he held my hand. "It's not good news, but it's nothing to be sorry for. If I had to catch sex cooties, I'm glad they were your sex cooties. Besides, he's been gone for a long time; you or I probably would have noticed something by now if we had it. It's going to be okay."

"I GAVE YOU VD!!!!!" I screamed. "Right now, little microbe gonorrheas could be lining up and down your wingding, waiting for the signal to stab you with little, tiny VD spears of pain, ready to unlock the gates of discharge! Don't you understand? I've made us statistics! 'Ten percent of the population has a drinking problem'—sure, count me in. 'Fifty percent of all smokers smoked their first cigarette in the field behind the high school when they were fourteen'—absolutely, I'm there. But 'One hundred percent of all whores will infect their very nice and understanding boyfriends with the red bumpies that supposedly make boys cry when they pee'—no, thank you. I don't want to be a card-holding member in the STD club."

My poor boyfriend had no idea what to do, and instead of taking a hold of the situation that was at hand, he panicked and allowed the control to spin out of the room like a dust devil in a trailer park. The poor man just lost it, started chewing off his own foot and most likely an arm or two.

"We'll get checked out, don't worry about it," he said, trying to calm me down. "And although I was going to save this for after the cutlets to see what meat product you had fried up for dessert, I'll just say it now: Let's get married."

I just looked at him. "That is not funny," I pouted. "Please don't tease me right now. I think I just felt my cervix shrivel up and crack."

"I'm serious," he said adamantly. "Let's get married."

"Did you hear me? I said I GAVE YOU VD!" I yelled. "Crotch rot! Peter poison! Weeping weenie! I have soiled you with a dirty man's sick! Who knows what tomorrow will bring—herpes, crabs, scabies? I mean, it turns out that I was involved with some pretty skanky characters—we're talking Renaissance-fair people, you know! That's like the *monarchy* of skank! In some cities, that's almost like homeless!"

"In most cities, that *is* homeless," my boyfriend said. "But I think we should get married. Especially now. I mean, if we can make it through this, a late electricity bill will be nothing. Starvation will be a laughing matter. Eviction will be a piece of cake. I mean, YOU GAVE ME VD!!!! Things don't get much stickier than this."

"God, it better not, or you'd better quarantine me," I agreed. "You're serious?"

"I'm serious," he confirmed, and then all of a sudden, agony filled his face, his body doubled over, and he screamed.

"What's the matter? What's the matter?!!" I panicked.

"Oh my God!" he cried shrilly. "Oh my God! My weenie is weeping! Weeping weenie!! WEEPING WEENIE!!!"

"Fine fine fine!!" I shouted. "Yes, this tramp will marry you!"

"Well, thank you, that's the answer I was looking for," he said, standing up straight, and then he smiled. "Actually, this will work out great. Maybe we can knock out both the VD and blood tests all at the same time!"

"I can't believe this," I said in a veil of happiness. "When I woke up this morning, I was just a below-average girl, but by the end of the day, I'm a fiancée with diseased genitals! And just think, I thought I scared you away for good when I fixed your paper jam and the booger came popping out of my nose."

"What are you talking about?" he said, looking rather puzzled. "I never saw a booger, but when you leaned over to fix the paper jam, I saw that you were fulfilling one of your job duties by leaving your bra at home. I saw your boob, and that's when I knew I loved you. I'm pretty sure it was the firmer one."

The Fat Bride Is Not
a Happy Magic Marker

Maybe it was my mistake.

Maybe I shouldn't have said anything at all.

I was getting dressed after my gynecologist lifted my hood and checked out my engine for signs of gonorrhea, and I just happened to mention it.

I was slightly concerned that, if I had contracted the creeping crud as my ex-boyfriend's ex-girlfriend informed me, it might have implications for my reproductive future.

"Don't worry about children now," my doctor said as she laughed mockingly at me. "You're not even married."

"I'm getting married . . . soon," I explained hesitantly. "And I don't want to have a newborn when I'm so old that we can sleep in cribs next to each other."

She laughed even harder.

"Let's wait and see if your marriage works out first," she scolded me. "It's no fun being a single parent."

Her comment felt like the slap of my mom's flip-flop to the side of my head. *What?* I thought as I looked at her. What *did you just say?* My mother is the only one who has the right to pop my self-esteem with a harpoon like that. You don't have that right! You've only seen me naked! The only right that gives you is to talk about me behind my back to other guys at the bar! My doctor made me feel like I was fifteen.

"And," she continued brazenly, "you shouldn't let your biological clock dictate when you have children."

OH NO, my mind yelled at her. Why pay any attention to that silly old biological clock? No, I'll just bring it to you to fix when it shoots out of me like a rocket and lands at my feet, how's that? Hopefully it will happen when you're giving me a Pap smear!

I suddenly felt like I was ten.

"I'm not letting that dictate when I'm going to have children—"

"Besides, you're too chubby to have children. You've gained twenty pounds since last December," she said, cutting me off in midsentence.

Too chubby to have children?

Then she said, motioning with her hands around her abdomen, "You'd have a hard time with all of *that* against your ovaries."

All I could think was, in a five-year-old's voice: (GASP) YOU ARE SUCH A BITCH!

So, okay, to be completely honest, I *knew* I had gained weight, it was *obvious* to me when I couldn't fit into certain items of clothing anymore. Rest assured, however, that I *didn't* have to pay someone to rev up a tractor to haul me out of bed in the morning.

She headed for the door, but before she left, she stopped in front of me, poked me in the belly, and said, "Just quit eating Twinkies and junk food."

I will not cry, I told myself, this devil woman will not make me cry.

She's just a bad lady, I told myself as I struggled valiantly to hold back my tears and the desire to pummel her bloody and pulpy with my fat rolls and my jiggly-wiggly thighs. She's a bad lady. A bad lady! And some day, a Hostess truck full of fresh bakery products will hit her and flatten her like a rug.

I finished getting dressed and rushed out of the room as fast as my fat, fleshy, stumpy little legs would carry me, and I went right up to the front counter where I promptly wrote her a big, fat, bad check in retaliation.

Then, I quickly escaped to the safety of the parking lot, the ground violently seizing with every step I took, where I jumped into my car and raced home.

"How did it go?" my boyfriend asked when I walked in the door.

"My doctor called me FAT," I shrieked.

"Are you okay, though?"

"I'M FAT," I shrieked again as I ran like a brachiosaurus down the hall and threw myself on the bed.

"You are not fat," my boyfriend asserted. "You look fine."

"Really?" I whined. "Do you really think so?"

"Well, honey, we eat nothing but assorted fried meats, mostly accompanied by some sort of butter sauce and occasionally cheese," he confessed. "You know, I've put on some weight, too."

"But I was plumping you up with cutlets so no other girls would find you attractive," I wept. "Just the typical 'pig to slaughter' tactic, nothing out of the ordinary. I would have stopped before you became freakish in size. It was working so well, and now my plan has backfired! Now I'm the fat one!"

"You're not fat," my boyfriend said again. "Some of your angles just have rounded corners now."

"I don't want to be a fat bride," I sobbed.

I went to work the next day and told everybody at the magazine what happened. I bequeathed my three-pound, neighborhood-size box of Oreos to Meg and Laura, the editors who sat across from me, and left my Hostess variety pack to Troy, the editor who sat next to me.

Both Laura and Meg said they understood my pain.

"I have to go on a diet, too," Laura said sadly.

"I know," Meg agreed. "Look at this roll when I sit down."

Meg then demonstrated her girth when she hunched way over in her chair until her head was basically resting on her knees.

"LOOK!" she cried enthusiastically, pointing to her middle. "Can you see it?"

Frankly, I didn't see a damn thing. Although Meg was one of my closest friends and I dearly loved her, I wanted nothing more than to ram an entire Death by Chocolate cake right down her throat, because that girl hasn't gained a single ounce since she stopped wearing undershirts.

Laura, too, joined the game and slumped down in her chair.

"Look at my roll! Look at my roll!" she yelled, pinching a wrinkle of skin that was smaller than what I can pinch on the back of my hand.

"Look at *my* roll when I sit down!" Anna shouted.

"NO, look at *my* roll when I sit down!" Rexia yelled back.

"SHUT UP!" I screamed. "Shut up about your roll! You all weigh as much as my leg! I have that roll in pairs all over me, and they don't go away when I stand up!"

They both stopped their Cirque du Soleil contortionist exercises and stared at me.

"This morning, I was on the potty after I got out of the shower, and I looked down," I confessed to them. "I know better than to do that, and I tell myself, 'Don't look down, don't look down,' but I did, and I realized that I'm in the body of a white, hairless gorilla. Come see me in Rwanda, I'm a friend of Dian Fossey's."

In Meg's motherly, concerned way, she tried to console me.

"Oh, dear," she started, stroking my hair. "PUV. Puffy Upper Vagina. That is a curse, now, isn't it? But I have a nice story to tell you. There was a chubby girl in my class, and she used to get made fun of all the time. Then, one day, she said something that I'll never forget. She turned around and told the skinny girls who were making fun of her, 'I'd rather be a happy Magic Marker than a toothpick with boogers on it.'"

Oh my God.

"Who is the Magic Marker in this scenario?" I asked. "I'm the Sharpie, aren't I, Meg? I am the Sharpie and you and Laura are the toothpicks, huh?"

"Troy's a happy Magic Marker, too," Meg offered.

This method of consoling, however, rarely works. Because you know what happens when you tell a fat person they're FAT? Well, they get sad and then they eat a cookie. They get sad and then they eat a doughnut. They get sad and then they eat a pizza. And then, the next day after you've called them fat because you "love them and want them to get healthy," THEY'RE FATTER. If you want a chunky to gain some skinny ground, tell them they look nice. Tell them that they look slimmer despite the obvious bad choice of the horizontal-stripe capri pants. Give them something to work with, something to build on.

"I want my Oreos back," the fat bride, who was no happy Magic Marker, huffed. "And only Troy and I get to eat them!"

"That's fine," Laura said as she handed over the cookie bag with both hands. "I'm still full from my breakfast of rice cakes and carrot sticks."

"And I just ate a *whole* grapefruit," Meg admitted. "If I even look at a cookie, I think I may burst!"

The next day, I decided to go on a diet, and packed Laura- and Meg-type things to eat at work, and when I showed Troy my lunch, he didn't even recognize any of the food groups in it.

He, on the other hand, had ordered himself a magnificent ham and cheese sub on a beautiful white, shiny roll, and his sandwich had *mayonnaise* on it.

It was the most beautiful thing I had ever seen.

And then I peered over his majestic sandwich and spied his gorgeous side of potato salad and the brick of carrot cake he had for dessert.

I opened my Tupperware bowl of tomatoes and sat at my desk. I couldn't help it.

"Hey! Magic Marker!" Troy yelled at me. "Quit looking at my food. You're only hurting yourself!"

I was suckling on my boring tomatoes when my phone rang, and who was it but the doctor who had caused me all of this agony in the first place.

"This is a follow-up call to your last visit," she said. "Your test results were normal."

The tomato dropped out of my mouth. "You mean I'm not fat?" I cried gleefully. "I can go back to eating things that have flavor and that bring me an unparalleled joy and deliver a comfort as no other activity can? Oh, thank you, Doctor! Thank you! Troy, give me half of that goddamned sandwich before I break your fat little arm!"

"No, you are still quite overweight," my doctor said. "Although you are free from the sexually transmitted disease known as gonorrhea."

"Oh," I stuttered loosely. "Oh, that's good news, that's great, thank you."

"It would be a prudent idea if you employed the aid of prophylactics during your sexual encounters to prevent this kind of problem in the future," she remitted.

"I'm getting married soon, so that won't be a problem," I stammered.

"You came in for a test, so obviously it is a problem," my doctor informed me. "Good marriages are hardly built on such foundations."

By that time I had had it, and I guess it was the hate that only hunger can cause in me, because in a moment, it all came rolling out in one, grand purge.

"You really don't know what you're talking about," I said as I reached for Troy's sandwich. "My boyfriend will totally still want to marry me even if I don't have VD! And maybe you think you can talk to people as if you were getting instructions straight from God's stethoscope, but I'll tell you one thing—not even God can help you cash this happy Magic Marker's check."

And then I took a big, splendid biteful of ham and cheese.

Hair of the Dog

Right according to plan, the moment my poor future mother-in-law opened her front door, she looked at me as if she had just seen me slide down a brass pole and shake my bare hips to a Nazareth song as a fat biker rewarded me by sticking a buck in my thong.

It was absolutely horrible.

And I suppose she had every right. There I was with my bleached and pink and purple hair; what else did I expect? Certainly, I'm sure, she expressed a sigh of relief that I hadn't just been on the news for diddling the president or a congressman, so things could have been worse, but still. I was far from Julia Roberts, even as a hooker in *Pretty Woman*.

When the ghastly moment passed, my boyfriend's mother bravely put on her best smile and invited me in.

After all, it was Christmas Day.

Frankly, I just wanted to find the bathroom and stay there, and I probably would have, had my new in-laws not thought that my absence was due to snorting a pound of cocaine rather than bone-chilling fear.

"I don't understand your friend's hair," I learned later that my boyfriend's sister said. "Why is it so many colors? And so unbrushed? I've only seen homeless people with that kind of hair."

"I used to have purple hair," my boyfriend reminded her. "And the knotty parts are just a couple of dreads; they're supposed to be there."

"Why is she wearing cowboy boots? Is she in the rodeo?" the other sister inquired.

"People wear combat boots who aren't in the army," my boyfriend reminded them.

"And this is the girl, Gloria, that you've been seeing?" they asked.

"No, this is the girl, Laurie, that I'm going to *marry*," he reminded them.

"Oh," they all said.

I really tried to put on a good show, to smile, to act pleasant, chew with my mouth closed, all of that stuff. I even retired the red lipstick for one day and switched to the Saucy Mauve that I had left over from my duty as my sister's bridesmaid.

In a kind maneuver to make me feel like I was part of the family, my future mother-in-law took me upstairs and asked if I'd help her wrap some last-minute gifts, a duty I couldn't have been more grateful for. It would permit me a few minutes out of the spotlight, I thought as I wrapped and followed her instructions for which tags went on which presents, enough time for them to get used to me, and now maybe the children wouldn't cry or ask if I was a witch when they saw me come back down the stairs.

As I returned with the wrapped gifts, my boyfriend met me on the landing.

"This is horrible, they hate me," I told him as I handed over some of the presents. "I think I'd rather have my next Pap smear broadcast over satellite TV or have my credit report published in the paper or just about anything than go back in there."

"It's fine, it's really fine," he said. "They seemed to like you a whole lot more when I told them you weren't pregnant."

"Oh, good, good," I said, nodding my head. "They think I'm Courtney Love, don't they?"

"Listen, you're wearing a bra, aren't you?" he whispered. "Because somebody said something about maybe seeing a boob . . ."

"Yes!" I whispered back. "Of course I'm wearing a bra! You know we have to wear bras at the magazine because if we don't, the police surveillance team might mistake us for one of the porno people making movies in the office downstairs from us!"

"Just checking," he said. "Just checking. Keep your arms crossed, just in case. Okay, are you ready to open presents?"

"No," I answered honestly. "But I wasn't ready to be the boob-flashing rodeo witch that I apparently am, so let's just go."

The present-opening began, and with the paper tearing and the kids squealing, for a moment, everything seemed okay as I sat back with crossed arms and watched.

"Wow, thanks, Mom," my boyfriend said as he held up his gift. "A Snow White video!"

"Thanks, Mom!" his sister said excitedly, holding up a pair of pearl earrings. "They're beautiful!"

"Aren't . . . those the earrings I asked for?" his other sister stuttered.

"I didn't have this on my list, but I guess we could use it," her husband said as he poked at what looked like a nursing bra. "I know I've gained a couple of pounds, but do I really need it? Tell me honestly."

"If anyone unwraps a gun, I'm calling first dibs," my boyfriend's brother asserted.

Everyone looked very confused except for my future mother-in-law and me. I already knew what had happened, and against all odds, no matter how impossible it seemed, I had completely destroyed the family's holiday even further than I had when they thought I was a pregnant, homeless stripper with knotted hair.

In my haste, in my stress, in my panic, I had apparently stuck the wrong tags on the wrong gifts, damaging the gift exchange, and as a result, a three-year-old was handling a Leatherman tool with about eight different knives on it, two sisters were about to rumble under the Christmas tree, a gun was possibly in our midst, and it was suspected that a coveted Diaper Genie was hiding somewhere under a tag with the phantom Gloria's name on it.

"I'm so sorry," I professed over and over again. "I am so sorry. I don't know how this happened. I am really, really sorry."

It was then that my boyfriend's nephew, a frisky, one-year-old toddler, waddled up to me and immediately went straight to second base, making a far quicker move than his uncle ever did. I didn't know exactly what to do, so I just sat there, trying to smile as he grappled at my right boob and trying to pretend I didn't have a baby feeling me up.

"Oh, he must be hungry," his mother said as she laughed and pulled him off me.

"Wow," I said lightly. "I've never been mistaken for a snack bar before."

"Here," my boyfriend's brother-in-law said as he laughed and tossed me his nursing bra. "I think this is probably for you."

They all laughed, and I laughed, too. When I looked at my boyfriend's mother, I saw that she was chuckling as well, and when she finally looked at me, she winked.

Dreading the Wedding

My friend Aaron has always been brutally honest with me. One night at Long Wong's, he looked at me and shook his head.

"You know," he started, "if anyone had ever said to me last year, 'Hey, Aaron, in twelve months, Laurie Notaro is going to quit smoking and get married,' I would've punched them right in the mouth and yelled, 'Hey, buddy, that's my *friend* you're talking about!'"

I quit smoking on purpose, when I thought I had cancer, but it just turned out to be a puffy Cheeto stuck in my throat. I didn't, however, set out to get married. I wasn't one of those girls who dreamed of her wedding day every time she closed her eyes, or who got a subscription to *Modern Bride* on her sixteenth birthday, or that could, at any given point in her life, recite the names of the girls who had made the final cut for her bridesmaids' squad.

So my boyfriend and I really had no idea what to expect. We were babies in the world of bridal registries and fairs, of caterers and florists, of boutiques and videographers; we were innocents. All I knew was what I had seen my sister go through the year before as she prepared for her wedding, and it wasn't pretty. My mother had only recently begun to sleep more than an hour a night and had just stopped walking around with the palm of her hand attached to her forehead, saying to no one in particular, "If you stop speaking to so-and-so and his wife, it will save your father and me thirty-five dollars and seventy-eight cents a head, which is what it's costing us to feed your rotten friends, who probably won't give you anything more for a wedding gift than movie tickets."

We set the date for our wedding for the following March, giving us more than a year to prepare for it. And, on a brave day a week after the "You're Fat Although Your Puffy Private Parts Appear to Be Disease-Free" incident, I went to my parents' house to break the news. I felt it was best if I went alone. Although I was twenty-nine, had graduated from college, and had a job, I felt like I was a promiscuous thirteen-year-old who had to tell her parents that her science teacher had knocked her up during a classroom experiment. With twins.

I don't know why I felt this way; the only conclusion I could come to was that I was raised as a Roman Catholic, a religion in which guilt plays a larger role than God. The only comfort I had in telling Mr. and Mrs. Notaro that their daughter was getting married was that my mother would be relieved that I would be in the presence of some sort of religious official, and, against all odds, it wasn't for a exorcism.

"I have something to tell you," I said to them after I had taken a deep breath and sat them both down.

"Oh my God, you're gay. She's gay. I told you she was gay," my mother immediately spit out. "You watched that goddamned *Ellen* show one too many goddamned times!"

"Nope, I'm not gay," I proclaimed. "And that's the good news! Isn't that good news? And here's more! I'm getting married next year."

"Hello, insomnia, my old friend," she said, her hand immediately flying up to her head. "Another wedding. Jesus, Mary, and Joseph, where's the Tylenol? If you were gay, you'd have to pay for this yourself, you know. If new neighbors move in next door to you, don't talk to them. If someone new starts at your work, you'd better ignore them. I'm not paying thirty-five dollars and seventy-eight cents a head for people we don't even know!"

The following weekend, the four of us, my boyfriend and I and my parents, attended five weddings we weren't invited to, to scout for possible wedding sites. I've never seen so many fat, permed bridesmaids stuffed into peach taffeta in all my life. I watched in horror as one groom lifted his new bride's dress over her head and took her garter off with his tongue and teeth; as another groom smashed the wedding cake into his bride's face so hard she had to blow her nose to get the frosting and little bits of strawberry out; and as another newly married couple blatantly shoved their tongues down each other's throat when anyone so much as knicked a glass with a spoon. The true horror came, however, at the last wedding when my father returned from the buffet and he was *chewing*.

Weddings, I began to understand, were vile, filthy things when they ran amuck.

That was the day I started to comprehend the phenomenon known as Dreading the Wedding. You see, when a girl becomes engaged, a transformation takes place and she becomes a prenuptial monster, crying at insurance commercials, picking out Las Vegas showgirl costumes for her bridesmaids and any five-year-old girl who happens to wander into her field of vision. If her mother lives in the same city, she has the potential and the actual, physical need to injure people. She torments everyone around her self-absorption bubble, sucking any passersby into her lair of white tulle as soon as they innocently ask, "So, how are the wedding plans going?" The victims, if they survive, escape the lair without a large percentage of their souls, then immediately adopt fifteen cats from the pound, buy several polyester/nylon-blend cardigans, and never leave their apartments again. If you always wondered how those people ended up like that, now you know. Once you've been exposed to that kind of fright, the world is forever a changed place, full of nothing but danger and brides.

The last wedding venue we looked at that day seemed to be perfect as long as we could turn off the noisy waterfall that tumbled at one end of the garden; it was a great location, with plenty of parking, we could bring our own booze, and we had the option of outdoor and indoor spaces.

"Oh, you're going to need that," my mother said. "It's going to rain that day, I'll tell you right now."

Because we wanted to have the wedding outside, she was convinced that not only was it going to rain that day, it was going to hail, and a typhoon, perhaps even a tsunami, would jump inland four hundred miles and the whole thing would be ruined. Just washed out. People would be swept away in violent waves and then drowned horribly. Almost everyone would die. The cake would be soggy. It would be a bad party.

So, in several days, when the date of our wedding was exactly a year away, I watched the sky, I felt the wind. It was a beautiful day, with a big yellow sun, the bluest sky available with the same white, puffed-up clouds you see only on toilet paper commercials. Perfect weather. And, when I was confident enough that afternoon, I called my mother.

"See?" I said, slightly proud of myself but far more pleased to have proved her wrong. "There's no storm today. There won't be a storm next year. Everything will be fine."

"The day isn't over yet," she said, taking a drag off her cigarette.

She was right, it wasn't. By the time the sun was starting to set, blue and black stormed the sky like bruises, the wind began to blow so hard that it hurt, and the temperature dropped twenty degrees in the same number of minutes.

I pushed the wedding back a week.

"You can't hide from the weather. It will hunt you down and find you," my mother responded. "There's no weather inside of a Catholic church, you know!"

Honestly, it wasn't the rain that scared me, but the fact that if I had seen an insurance commercial featuring an ill child or a house full of family memories burning right down to the ground at any point that day, I probably would have cried.

Naked with a Stranger

I already knew that no matter what transpired during that afternoon, it was going to end up in a fight.

A big fight, too, not a little fight where people just quit talking to each other, but a big fight that lands one or both participants either in the Madison Street jail or on an afternoon talk show.

I wondered if I still had a strong right hook; it had been years since I had needed to use it. It used to be good enough to leave a hell of a mark. This time, however, I had the feeling that it was gonna have to be pungent enough to knock out a couple of teeth.

My opponent had approximately twenty-two years more experience in man-to-man, hand-to-hand combat than I did, putting me at a definite disadvantage. She was an expert in pinching, open-hand slapping, hair-pulling, and Indian burns, and had also won the National Mark of Excellence Award by transforming a hairbrush into a lethal weapon. I knew all about that award. She received it after she beat the crap out of me on my eleventh birthday because I spit on my sister and then hit her in the leg with a dried-up dog turd.

The only advantage I could possibly have would be to try and stay calm. That was it, that was the only thing I could do. I knew damn well that my competitor could whip herself up into a whirling dervish in a matter of seconds, and if I kept my ability to reason, the advantage would be mine.

Then she called me on the phone.

"I'll be there in twenty minutes to pick you up," she said.

"Okay," I agreed, "I'll be ready."

"What condition are your armpits in?" she queried.

"Oh no," I protested. "I refuse. I am not shaving."

"Yes, you are."

"I don't have any razors," I reasoned. Stay calm, I told myself, keep the edge.

"I'll bring you one," she informed me. "The way you keep parts of your body is disgusting. Where did you learn these things? I raised you to shave. You can't let other people see you like that!"

"What do you mean?" I asked. "No one's coming in with me!"

"Oh yes," she said, and I could sense her smile widen on the other end of the phone. "Yes, they certainly do. They have to dress you."

"You didn't tell me that strangers were going to see me naked," I protested. "I don't want strangers to see me naked! I'm going to have to put on some underwear, and I don't even know if I *have* any."

I'm sure she believed that she was teaching me a lesson, but she wasn't. She was only proving that she could enforce her vetoing power only as a mother who was paying for her daughter's wedding could.

Today was going to be an important battle in the war of my wedding, the struggle over the bridal gown. Up until now, my mother had exercised her veto power in pretty much every area known to *Bride*'s magazine and we barely agreed on anything.

You see, in other places in the world, where weddings haven't become big business, getting married is easy. In Kenya, the father of the bride spits on the bride's head and on her breasts to demonstrate his good wishes, and as the bride departs, she does not look back for fear that she will turn to stone. All you need is some drool and an allegorical threat that a fair maiden will turn into a monolith and the wedding is a rampant success. The mother doesn't have time to figure out how to ruin the experience for her daughter.

But here, things are different. You need a ceremony, reception, a band, a DJ, invitations, favors, a caterer, a photographer, a florist, a baker, a videographer—the list doesn't end, ever. I believe my family is the current world-record holder for attending more weddings that we weren't invited to. As a result, I've crashed more receptions in one day than I did parties during my entire time as an undergraduate.

My mom, still fresh from planning my sister's wedding, had a pretty good idea of the way she wanted things to be and who she wanted to hire in this off-Broadway production. I thought that I might have some bargaining power since it was my wedding, but I was obviously using it incorrectly. The whole thought of the event would make my stomach burst into boiling ulcers, so I did the only thing I could do: I asked my shrink for $120's worth of advice.

"It's *your* wedding, Laurie," she stressed. "You're going to have to fight for what you want."

"I know, I know," I answered. "But it's beyond that. You don't understand."

"It can't be *that* bad," my therapist said. "Pick out certain things that are especially important to you, and focus on those. Something like your invitations, your dress, the place where the wedding will be."

"Yeah," I nodded, "except that I found out that my mom's been looking at places without me."

My therapist stopped for a moment, crinkled her brow, then sat back in her chair.

"In that case, you have only one option," she said slowly. "Give up. Surrender. You're fighting a losing battle. Try and concentrate on your honeymoon, then."

"You think I should give up? Just like that?" I stuttered. "Well, can you ask someone else, like one of your therapist friends? Can you ask them for advice?"

She just shook her head. It was obviously useless.

I was remembering that conversation when my mom pulled into the driveway. I could tell she was excited. She just kept honking the horn, over and over again. I locked the side door of the house and started walking toward the car. In less than half an hour, I thought to myself, I will be standing in front of a mirror in some bridal store, looking at my reflection and realizing that I look remarkably like a Judd or one of the Gabor sisters, dead or alive.

We got to the bridal shop.

My mother picked out the dresses she liked.

I got naked in a dressing room with a stranger.

But it was way worse than that. I had no hope of capturing any of the glamour of Eva, Ava, or Ova when all of that white satin came tumbling over my head. I didn't even have the charm of one of their poodles.

When I came face-to-face with the real-life image of Laurie in a wedding dress, the first thing I thought was, "Realistically, what are my chances of dying in a Dust Devil–related home-liposuction attempt?"

The second thing I thought was "Can I hire a stand-in?"

And the third thing I thought was "I'm already that monolith."

My mother, on the other hand, saw something different. She most likely had the wrong glasses on, but in that mirror she didn't see Agnes Gooch or a girl crammed into a wedding dress so tight she looked like a Price Club–size white satin sausage. My mother saw a bride.

I saw razor burn.

"You'll look beautiful," my mother said. "Once you brush your hair."

"You look good," the saleslady added. "It makes your boobs perky."

"Oh, thanks," I answered. "I thought only a crane or five thousand dollars could do that."

"You look so pretty," my mother reiterated. She smiled.

She knew what she was doing.

I couldn't fight with someone who was telling me that I was fetching, perky, or relatively attractive.

She won the battle, that day.

I never even got to form a fist.

The Suck of Bridal G-Force

I will admit there was a moment that I really did get sucked into a bridal black hole. In a way, you can hardly help it. After spending months of leafing through ten pounds of wedding magazines every single time you come back from the grocery store, your mind becomes a little soft and very open to suggestion. After you've flipped through the newest issues of *Modern Bride*, *Bridal Guide*, *Bride's*, *Martha Stewart Weddings*, *InStyle Weddings*, *Bride Again*, and *Encore Bride*, you will honestly believe that you will look exquisite walking down the aisle dressed as a lemon meringue pie, or even more tragic, a coconut macaroon.

Bridal magazines propagate faster than mosquitoes. Every time I went to pick up a stick of margarine or a box of tampons, there on the shelf was a brand-new issue of the same magazine I bought yesterday. In hindsight, I am fully convinced that it's actually the same, exact magazine, but that the publishers supply retailers with thirty different covers each month, and when the one on the shelves is sold, the quickest bag boy on staff runs to the supply room immediately to fetch the next version of the magazine with the new cover. It wouldn't be a difficult scam at all; every magazine has the same awful dresses that make you believe that the Civil War era really is back in fashion and that if you want a gaggle of bridesmaids that could double for Suellen O'Hara, Melanie Hamilton, and Aunt Pittypat on Halloween, that is your God-given right as a bride, and anyone who tries to talk you out of it is nothing less than the devil. All sport the same, limp stories with headlines like "Flatware: An Investigative Report," "Is Your Coffeemaker Meeting Your Needs?" and "The Truth Behind 200-Thread-Count Sheets." Bridal magazines are kind of like OxyContin for the ivory satin/tulle crowd, and when you get down to it, I believe they are the number-one cause of why it is easier to reason with a crack addict than it is an engaged woman.

Because of bridal magazines and an emphatic endorsement from my mother, I became convinced that not creating a bridal registry was nothing short of bestial.

"If you don't go and register this very minute," my mother warned, "I'll tell you right now that every present you open will be candlesticks and salt and pepper shakers. And you can't build a home on that! If you don't believe me, there was a very good article in one of your magazines called 'Flatware: An Investigative Report' that you should read. You ever try eating stroganoff with a candlestick? Have you? Yeah, that's what I thought. Then *register*."

Haunted by the vision of trying to cut into a filet mignon with a salt shaker for the rest of eternity, I grabbed my boyfriend and we embarked on picking out stemware, washcloths, casual dinnerware, and lots of things we didn't want but could return for cash or credit, since there was a great pair of cowboy boots I had my eye on in the shoe department. In effect, the entire ordeal was nothing short of an engagement hazing/endurance test. It took us two days, rotating in shifts, to pick out all of the essential things we were going to need or risk our marriage eroding into a miserable and dismal failure. Every choice was laced with trepidation and chance. Who knew if the double old-fashioned juice glasses could be the unraveling of our love or if the villain was really the etched goblets? You never knew. *You never knew.* I didn't even know the truth behind two-hundred-thread-count sheets and if three hundred was better or worse, and there I was, picking out things that were supposed to last a lifetime.

I realized I had crossed a line when I was standing in the towel department and found myself shouting across the aisle to my boyfriend—who was seeking well-deserved slumber on a bed the size of a hot dog meticulously vignetted in Ralph Lauren's Avery Cafe bed linens—"Why are we even going through the motions of this wedding if we aren't getting the full-size bath sheets? What is the point?"

Bridal black hole. Sucked right in. Fortunately, I was able to pull out of it after I received an invitation to a bridal fair at the same department store a week after we registered. The lure was free gifts. I figured if I wasn't going to be a beautiful bride, I might as well get some free stuff by just being a bride in the first place, and I talked my unfortunate maid of honor and best friend since third grade, Jamie, into going with me.

As the loot was handed out, we saw one girl tackle another for a free Wedgwood gravy boat. I saw a bride-to-be and her maid of honor work an unsuspecting lone bride like grifters, trying to make her trade her Lenox crystal ring-holder gift for their package of thank-you cards. I saw a girl erupt into tears when she opened what looked like a jewelry box that really held a pen with an attachment for a big, nasty feather. And I watched all of them circle around me like raptors when I won the shower cake as Jamie held them at bay with lit aromatherapy candles she grabbed from a nearby display.

It was enough to make me go home, grab the closest wheelbarrow, gather up approximately fourteen hundred pounds of bridal magazines, and dump them straight into the gaping black hole of our recycling bin.

Don't Drink the Kool-Aid

We had run into a snag.

Neither my boyfriend nor I had been to a church in years and had no one to marry us. Although one of our friends swore he was an ordained minister and would perform the ceremony, we changed our minds when we found out what kind of medication he was on.

After some searching, I found a minister in the phone book and made the call. Assuring me of what a great ceremony he performed (including a portion in which the bride and groom high-five each other), he then informed me that he was busy on our date and that he would refer me to one of his colleagues.

That's how we found Ellen.

Ellen called, and told us that she ran a church on the west side of town. She suggested that we come down to the service the following Sunday to see if we liked each other. I agreed. There couldn't be any harm in that.

On Sunday, we got up early, took showers, and made sure we were both wearing clean underwear, even if both pairs were my boyfriend's. We ironed his shirt and got ready for church.

With the address in hand, we set off for Ellen's place. We were both pretty hungry, though, and stopped for some McEgg thing on the way there, ordering as much as we could with the five dollars we had on us. We had finished gobbling everything just about the time we reached the street the church was on. We made the turn.

There, behind a wall of blooming oleander bushes, was a parking lot, and as we pulled into it, we noticed that the layout of the place was kind of odd. Scattered about the edge of the lot were numerous little houses, perhaps seven or eight in all, and then what was obviously a main hall. Our car was one of three in the lot.

"This doesn't look like a church," I said quietly.

"But it sure does look like a compound," my boyfriend replied.

"It's a cult," I said adamantly. "It's a cult, they're trying to recruit us. It's like Little Guyana or a Branch Davidians franchise. Great. Cult people. Our minister is a Jim Jones. '*Come, children, come, don't be afraid.*' "

"Well, what do you want to do?" he asked me.

"I want to leave," I answered, looking over both shoulders. "Unless they've already surrounded us."

"You made an appointment with her," he argued. "I think we should go in. You said she sounded nice."

"Honey, you capture more cult people with honey than you do with vinegar. What do you think she should have said, 'Hey, did you ever feel the urge to become the sixth child bride of a balding, overweight man with a perspiration problem and big pores, because I can hook you up by sundown'! You know that cult people always make the new recruits drink their own pee!" I reminded him, but he was already out of the car.

"It can't hurt to see," he insisted.

"Okay, okay." I gave in. "Your choice. But if anyone hands you Kool-Aid or a loaded rifle, just back away slowly and say nicely, 'No, thank you,' and if you see any children dressed in fatigues, don't say a word, just run to the car."

We walked through the doors of the main hall, into a room

about as big as a classroom. Several rows of metal folding chairs were set up, occupied by a variety of about fifteen people. In the air hung the undeniable fragrance of old coffee and nicotine residue, a sure signal that cleanliness wasn't as next to godliness as you'd like to think around these parts. As I looked around, I had the undeniable feeling that I was the Mary Poppins of this group.

Yep. Mixed-up, brainwashed cult people. Suddenly, the high-fives seemed perfectly acceptable, even downright *cool*, as did the Wave or even the Jerry Springer chant, "Go Jerry! Go Jerry! Go Jerry!" My mother could handle that after we said our vows, I convinced myself, especially if we let her *start* the Wave.

As soon as we each took a seat, the piano player attacked the keys with the chords of "We Shall Overcome," and instructed the congregation to come to the front of the room, hold hands in a circle, and sing. In what was clearly an invasion of my personal space, I joined hands with perfect strangers and sang what little I knew of the song, swaying involuntarily with my hands above my head, my right in the clutch of a man wearing an eye patch and my left grasped tightly by a woman missing both her eyeteeth. For all I knew, in an hour I could be married to Bluebeard and forced to follow the orders of his first wife, The Whistler.

When we very gladly and happily returned to our seats, a basket was passed around (a part of church I had completely forgotten about), and before it got to us, I was able to scavenge the thirteen cents that was left over from our McBrunch and tossed it into the collection. I didn't feel so bad after I took a peek in the basket and realized that we were apparently the high rollers in this "church," being that the parishioners donated what they could afford to sacrifice. Along with the bounty of our thirteen cents, the basket boasted a half-smoked GPC cigarette, an origami bird created from a gum wrapper, several Canadian pennies, and what looked suspiciously like a rewrapped cough drop.

The lady I assumed was Ellen stood up and began delivering her sermon. Short and squat with eyes that said she had done some hard living, she began talking in a soft voice about how people should accept other people for who they were, just like Jesus did, and, as a matter of fact, if He were to come back to Earth right now, He'd feel much more comfortable at this church with the drug addicts and over-the-limit offenders than he would in Scottsdale with the hoity-toity people eating raw fish at a sushi bar.

"A-men, Sister Ellen, the Lord is *every* man! *Every* man!" one particularly invigorated churchie stood up and proclaimed. "*Every* man fights his own demons, like my own enemy, cocaine!"

"And the temptation of drink!" another man yelled.

"And the crack pipe!" The Whistler barely rattled.

It was then that I understood. We weren't in a compound, and we weren't about to be brainwashed. No one was going to give me a gun and start calling me Tonya. I wasn't going to drink my own pee. We were simply at a rehabilitation center. A nonvoluntary, court-appointed rehab center. For these folks, it was singing and dancing and praising the Lord or wrestling the last scrap of shit wipe from their cellmates in the Big House while using their metal feeding tray as a shield. It turns out that we didn't need to wear clean underwear, after all. We were sitting in a meeting of Junkies for Jesus.

We met Ellen afterward, and I decided that I liked her just as long as she didn't bring her commonwealth to our wedding for a free meal, despite the entertainment value of an honest-to-God freak show, and the fact that if Jesus chose to return to Earth, He might show up at my wedding, looking for His "every man" peeps. Then she gave me her card, which I have never, to this day, shown my mother.

It read, neatly in black and white: "Reverend Ellen, A Spiritual Solution To Addictions."

Dead Bride Walking

I was getting married in eleven days.

I had spent the last year planning, scouting, gluing, and stressing for our wedding. Yesterday I had five months to finish getting my shit together, but this morning it transformed into a matter of hours.

I thought that I might even need to speak to a chaplain.

When it comes time to do it, I wanted to ask him, will it be painless? Will I feel anything? Will it be peaceful or will I suffer?

Will I still be worrying that the ex-boyfriend and ex-girlfriend, respectively at tables six and fifteen, will end up slugging it out? Will anyone take a piss in public at the reception? Will anyone have sex at my wedding? Will my mother throw anyone out for having a potty mouth? Will my missing-in-action bridesmaid actually show up? How many guests are going to bring people who weren't invited and where do I seat them? How big is the chance that I will burst into a molten lava menstrual flow as I walk down the aisle?

Is he actually going to marry me?

What happens if he dies within the next eleven days—do I have to send back all the gifts? Will any one of the waiters be somebody I've slept with in a past life? Will I remember to wear underwear that day? Will my mother and I be speaking by then? Have I gained too much weight to fit into my dress? Is it going to rain?

Will I have a big pimple on my neck, or a whitehead on the side of my nose that no one will tell me about? If I end up crying like a ninny, can I do it in a way that people will think I'm choking on a chunk of cheese or some chocolate? Will our three-year-old ring bearer pick his nose and then put the treasure back, a favorite habit of his, when he's standing at the altar?

Will the known kleptomaniac of the family try to steal the gifts, particularly the money bag? Will people I hate try to crash the reception, just to piss me off? Will the suspected retarded family member eat with his hands or use utensils? Is the chicken going to be fatty? Do I really need to shave or can I wear tights instead of hose? How much am I allowed to eat? Do I need to wear a girdle? How can I kiss my boyfriend without turning him into a transvestite? Can I light the candles without spilling wax on myself or setting my hair on fire? Is it too late to have liposuction on my chin? Have I turned into one of those beasts that have nothing to talk about but their wedding? What if I have to take the Big Poo?

Have all of the bridesmaids gotten their dresses altered? Will people who didn't RSVP show up anyway? Does anyone know how to complete a bow tie? Do I need a dowry? Will he marry me without one? What the hell is a dowry? Does it involve livestock? My family knows nothing about livestock or animal husbandry. How about my dog? Can she take the place of livestock in the dowry? Can I use my bra for the "something old" bit? Why did I allow my mother to buy the garter? It has *feathers* on it and a bell. Do I really have a mustache or is it just my bathroom light? Do I look like a sausage in my dress? If anyone throws rice, I know it's going to hit me in the eye and I'll have to keep that eye closed for the rest of the wedding, or make sure I bring an eye patch. Have I remembered *Modern Bride*'s three C's: Consideration, Communication, and Compromise?

Am I still mad at her or should I snub her at the reception? I

wonder if he is bringing that awful girl? What if I fall down? Is anyone going to do the "I object!" thing or will they hold their peace?
Will the groomsmen tape the words "Help Me!" on the bottom of
the groom's shoes? I'll have nothing to talk about when this whole
thing is over. Did I need to ask the Pope for permission? I forgot to
ask the Pope for permission. Is it my religion that steps on the
glass? What kind of glass? Does it have to be holy glass? Where do
you get holy glass? Can I just use a lowball? I hope no one plays
"My Love Does It Good." Do I have to admit to any felonies now?

After the reception, will my mother have to kick an unconscious
person, found lying under one of the tables, repeatedly, screaming, "Young man, it is time to go home! *Where are your friends?*"
What happens when he finally sees me naked with the lights on?
God, I'll have to unscrew every lightbulb from now until he gets
Alzheimer's and forgets what women are supposed to look like.
Did I give the Reverend the right directions and is she bringing a
date? Please don't let it be the guy swathed in army green swatting at imaginary flies or the junkie with the eye patch. If it is the
junkie, though, maybe I can borrow the patch temporarily if I am
maimed by the unexpected rice. What if I fart by accident? What if
I fart in front of everyone? Did I invite that person? I think I forgot
to invite that person. Oh God. I forgot to invite that person. What
if someone gets high in the parking lot and my mother sees him?
Will she call the police? Of course she'd call the police. She's my
mother.

Oh my God.

Oh my God.

Eleven days.

I'm a Dead Bride Walking.

"If You Get Divorced Within a Year, You Owe Your Father $35.78 a Dinner Times Two Hundred": Words of Wisdom on My Wedding Day

The morning of her wedding, there are some things that a bride is better off not knowing.

Really, it's true. You can exhaust yourself becoming prepared, tending to every minute detail, taking the proactive stance against any little, tiny thing that may possibly go wrong. But it's useless.

Because there is no precaution against fate.

And it's better when a bride doesn't know that. When she doesn't know that, at any second, forces she cannot understand, much less control, will swoop down from the heavens and kick her off-white, Italian-satin ass six ways from Sunday while the photographer is taking her picture at the same time.

I woke up on the morning of my wedding and embarked on my Preventative Measures Plan. If there was anything that scared me on my wedding day, it was the possibility that once I was up there in front of two hundred people and I became actively involved in vow-taking, I would be sucker-punched by an intestinal cramp that would demand an immediate escape to the ladies' room with a commemorative book of matches in hand. In other situations, sure, you can sneak away when a doody gremlin is tugging at your colon, but good luck when you have a leading role and your part is up next, although I was somewhat prepared to muddle through.

I've been onstage before. When I was nine, my dance school put on a recital for an old folks home, and right smack in the middle of our tap-dancing salute to the theme song from *The Sting,* an old man pushed his wheelchair to the front row, unzipped his fly, pulled what I understood to be an uncooked sausage out of his pants, and then peed all over the floor. At that age, I was completely unaware that men could even do that, and as I stared at the puddle in front of me, my little feet kept shuffling off to Buffalo as Judy Garland's voice shouted in my head, "Go ON with the show! Go ON with the show!" while the rest of my dance class burst into tears, walked off stage, or just plain sat down.

So to cut the digestive train off at the pass, I flipped open the box of Immodium AD, my best means of protection against The Big Poo. I popped two out of their foil bubble-pack tombs and chewed them mercilessly, then chowed down another one for good measure.

Step Two involved looking in the mirror, and what I saw amazed me. My face was clear. Absolutely clear. Although I had a Band-Aid in hand and had painstakingly constructed a far-fetched yet almost believable story about how members of a nearby killer-bee colony had expressed an attraction for my new honey-milk hand lotion (in case I had more than one zit, I could attribute the breakout to a swarm attack by the hive), I did not have a strawberry-size boil on my nose, neck, or chest that required makeup, bandaging, or immediate cosmetic lancing. My mother owed me five whole bucks.

Step Three in my Preventative Measures Plan consisted of using a flashlight and a mirror with magnifying properties only a surgeon would need to scan my chinny-chin-chin in a quest for devious little piggy hairs. I used to think that I had a very kind, sympathetic mirror, but I now lean toward the theory that I bought a defective one, because in my bathroom, I have a regular female jaw. Push me into the power of direct sunlight, however, and I have chin scrub fuller than Grizzly Adams's. Since I was getting married outside, my mandible foliage had the potential to be a deal breaker, so I had to reap the forest carefully with my trusted tweezers. I relied on my tweezers solely after my encounter with wax strips, which do not disclose in the instructions that repeated usage in the same area after about fifteen applications will indeed rip all remnants of testosterone and most of the skin cells right off your face, leaving exposed bone. I learned that lesson the hard way the night of our engagement party as I and my perfectly proportioned, square-shaped chin scab tried to act cute and engaged, while behind me, my invited guests were exchanging scenarios about how I may have acquired a rug burn in such a precarious and delightful spot.

In Step Four, I layered myself with so much padding that if I had been knifed in the gut by any of my boyfriend's ex-girlfriends or his mom, not so much as a drop would have seeped through to the other side. There was no way I was going to have to borrow a sweatshirt or cardigan to tie around my bustle on my day of all days.

This bride was prepared. She was all set.

Or so she thought.

It wasn't until I was watching the bridesmaids walk down the aisle to the music of the string quartet that I realized I was at my wedding. My betrothed was already up at the turned-off waterfall with Ellen, watching the procession.

I wasn't shaking, I hadn't cried, I wasn't stuttering or hissing, all of which were good signs, or at least symptomatic of the eight Midols I had recently swallowed. And here we were, I thought, four minutes into the wedding and everything was running smoothly. I smiled and took a deep breath. What was I worried about?

In forty seconds, I was walking down the aisle myself on the arm of my father, who had been either a very wise man and remained absolutely silent for the past year or had sold his tongue to pay for the ice sculpture. I don't believe he had talked to anybody, including his reflection, since we announced our engagement.

Suddenly, from overhead, an all-enveloping, powerful roar—the kind of roar that urges you to duck and seek cover—was being born above us, and as all two hundred heads looked up, they saw the nose, the windshield, and the pilots—one of whom looked like a guy I went to high school with who sold really bad pot in the darkroom of the yearbook office—of a 747 preparing to land.

It suddenly dawned on me that we were three miles from the airport, and it would have been impossible to be more directly in line with the north runway of the fifth busiest airport in the country and fifteenth busiest airport in the world.

Even I couldn't hear what Ellen was saying. The noise fell over us like a blanket, smothering everything: the courtyard, the guests, the turned-off waterfall, which would have been a whisper compared to the jet engines that were thundering above us in a deafening, rumbling roar. And no sooner had the jetliner taken its time to blast above us and then retreat than another one popped up, riding on the first one's heels.

Then a third plane arrived, and a fourth and a fifth, the aggregate roar lasting longer than the complete running time of the ceremony, including the scheduled musical performances, the photographic slide montage, grand finale, and encore.

Our beautiful wedding location was loaded with more airspace activity than Afghanistan. It couldn't have been louder if we had chosen to get married on an aircraft carrier.

Poor Reverend Ellen. Not even a lifetime of living in a compound with habitual offenders and felons or paying back her own debt to society could have prepared her for this situation. She may have had a spiritual solution to addictions, but her pockets of God were empty when it came to the noise level of a sonic boom. She tried to solve our dilemma by talking as fast as she could when we recognized the threat of approach, and squeezing in as much as possible, until she began to sound like an auctioneer.

"Stand fast in that hopeandconfidencehavingfaithinyourshared-destinyjustasstronglyasyouhavefaithinyourselvesandinoneanothertoday," Ellen said with a stretched smile just before she took a deep, scuba-dive breath and went back in. "Onlywiththisspiritcan-youforgeaunionthatwillstrengthenandendureallthedaysofyour-livesJesusIcoulduseadrinkrightnow!"

Even I wasn't sure which point in the wedding we were at—was I still single, was I loving, was I obeying, was I married, was it time for the fire baton twirlers to swing in on the trapezes?—I had absolutely no idea. I tried to utilize my therapist's advice and focus in on the positive, as in, "I HAVE NO CHIN HAIR, I HAVE A COTTON FIELD BETWEEN MY LEGS, AND I WON'T HAVE TO SHIT FOR A MONTH," but I was absolutely positive when I turned around for our march back up the aisle that I would see my now bald mother on a stretcher while a paramedic performed CPR. With every passing plane, she'd have pulled out another fistful of hair and another and another until there wasn't anything left for her to do but throw a hissy fit in such massive proportions that she would just plain knock herself out.

That's when I swore I heard an evil chuckle from the back row. If I did, I knew exactly where it came from. It was the same man who an hour before had yelled at Meg when she politely pulled the hand of the three-year-old ring bearer away from his nose, his finger buried deep inside.

"That's one of the best shots I had all day!" growled the videographer when Meg interrupted the booger taffy pull, although now he was making up for lost footage with his camera pointed directly toward the sky. It wasn't the first nasty thing he had done that day. I watched as he rolled his eyes when Meg hid bra straps and informed a groomsman that his fly was open as we were taking our wedding pictures, stuff that, no doubt, would be pure gold to the videographer after he sold our wedding video and cashed the check from the funniest-home-video show.

After the ceremony, he followed us around like a loser friend we couldn't shake. It took him forty minutes to set up the shot of us signing our marriage certificate when we should have been in the receiving line, and amazingly, the only part he clearly got on tape was when I was digging a morsel of a cocktail meatball out of my teeth with my tongue, which required so much concentration that I forgot to keep my engorged cutlet stomach sucked in. He told us when to eat. When to make the toast. When my new husband could kiss me. When we should cut the cake. When we could dance with each other and our parents. I looked up during dinner, and somehow, he had seated himself at my mother-in-law's table and was sitting next to her, with his camera turned off. He wasn't filming anything. He was stuffing his fat, nasty face with chicken Parmesan and au gratin potatoes.

His appearance was entirely misleading, and it took me a while to understand that, because although, yes, this man carried around a video camera and had something stuck in his ear, he was no videographer. No, no, no. What he really revealed himself to be was a professional Wedding Ruiner.

During dinner, I had to wrestle a hard roll out of the maid of honor's hand that was positioned and ready to be fired at his head.

"A roll can't hurt," Jamie argued as the bread turned to crumbs in between our fingers.

"I know, but the butter knife you had rammed through it *might*," I reminded her. "C'mon, I promised my parents that no one would sue them today!"

Craig, the best man, was behind her, ready to fling a steaming piece of roast beef, spiked on a fork, at the chewing target.

Maybe other newlywed couples had higher tolerance levels than we did, maybe they wanted someone else to take control of their wedding. But I didn't. I had spent a year planning details, and both my new husband and I knew what we wanted and when we wanted it. I didn't need the video man to poke me in the back with his finger and pronounce, "Hey. You're losing your crowd. You'd better throw your bouquet now or you can forget the whole thing."

I had known this man less than twenty-four hours, and in that

time, he disrupted our wedding more effectively than the unexpected appearance of an ex-girlfriend with a newborn baby. He
was so busy pushing us around, insulting the members of the
wedding party, and setting up shots of fake events to film a wedding that didn't exist that I never got to greet a majority of our
guests, let alone take stock of who was shoving centerpieces and
the remainder of the meatball pyramid into their purses.

The only time he truly left me alone was when I was with my
eighty-four-year-old grandfather, Pop Pop. Pop had come to the
wedding in a wheelchair because the medication for his cancer
left him a little dizzy, and a wheelchair seemed the best way to
make him mobile. I figured, hell, if I could have someone push me
around while I went from the meatball pyramid to the cheese
tower to the fondue station and it wasn't an expense my mother
made me pay for myself, I'd go for it. After all, isn't that how Liza
Minelli attended every milestone event in her life?

The DJ began playing one of his favorite Frank Sinatra songs,
and before Old Blue Eyes even belted out the second line, Pop had
thrown his lap blanket to the ground, wiggled out of his wheelchair, grabbed me from the head table, and spun me out to the
dance floor.

As he led me in the fox-trot, Pop tossed me around like a rag
doll to "Fly Me to the Moon," and while they looked on, most of
my husband's extended family were stunned. For them, it could
have only been a genuine act of God, even without the snakes or
an evangelist's palm-smack to the forehead. Minutes before,
some of them whispered to each other, the man who had been
confined to a wheelchair had not only freed himself from the
chains of his rolling prison and *walked* but now was *dancing*. There
wasn't a dry eye in the house. "It's a miracle, it's like Joseph Smith
and the seagulls," some of them said among themselves, but I
didn't want to ruin it for anybody by informing them, "The old
man's on *morphine*. You could ram a spear through his foot and
he'd still keep going. He's as numb as Robert Downey, Jr."

The videographer kept his distance until the dance was over, when he proceeded to torment me about taking the frigging garter off. He was sure to catch a wonderful shot of the drunkest, sweatiest man at the wedding as he unabashedly tackled the three-year-old ring bearer in a shameful yet successful effort to catch the damn thing. This was the same man who had marched around the reception, telling various people, including my parents, what "hot lovers" Italian women were and how the groom, whose name he did not know, was going to have to let the bride, whose name he also did not know, lead in bed, since she looked like she was more than familiar with the trail.

When we discovered that one of my husband's aunts was now parading around the reception with the garter stretched around her neck, we were also able to figure out that the horrible, drunk, sweaty man was her date.

He was vile, he was vulgar. He was so sweaty that he looked like he had just walked straight out of an adult bookstore, and as he shook his head to the music, droplets scattered as if he were a dog shaking out its coat after an especially wet bath. His head was like a sprinkler. As the sweaty guy contorted his body to make every letter corresponding to "YMCA" that was pumping out over the speakers, he sang along, pointed, and put on the same kind of show I was sure he did every Friday night at karaoke. He was at our wedding, feeding off of it like a virus, and all I could think was "I hope the check you wrote to us as a wedding gift clears my bank account before you die from the heart attack you're about to have on my dance floor."

The videographer, however, adored him, and found him such a great form of nonstop entertainment that he's in our wedding video more than either the bride or groom, *combined*. It's all documented as he dances, sings, and tells assorted guests, particularly my Nana, how that poor groom was probably not going to get a wink of sleep for the next week because of his hot and horny ball and chain.

Finally, after the videographer suggested that we stage a fake good-bye shot, I had my chance.

"Did you have a nice time?" I asked him. "Because you ate at my wedding, you drank at my wedding, you made an M with your arms with the human water fountain over there, so I'm thinking that you enjoyed yourself at my wedding, am I right?"

"Oh, sure," he said as he picked up the camera and started filming me. "I had a great time. Now, when you're waving good-bye to your crowd, look happy, but a little sad, like a clown. It would be great footage if you could get a couple of tears going."

"That's good, I'm glad you had fun," I continued. "But now it's my turn to have fun. See, to you, I'm just another chick in a white dress that you get to order around, but this is my wedding. I had to overcome A LOT to get here, including, but not limited to, singing with junkies, getting naked with strangers in dressing rooms, seven days straight of brushing dreads out of my hair, and a scare with VD. I would like to enjoy what is left of my wedding, but in order for that to happen, you must leave."

"I'm sorry, I don't understand," he said as he put the camera down. "I was paid to shoot this wedding."

"No, no, no, no," I said slyly as I wagged my finger in front of him. "You were only paid a *deposit*. That's only *half*. Since, however, you are a bastard and I hate you, I would suggest you leave the premises right now if you want to see the other half of your fee. And if you don't believe me, I wouldn't mind one bit if you called the district attorney's office or my gynecologist to see exactly how good I am at writing bad checks. It's just a shame that you won't be here to film yourself getting thrown out of my wedding, because so far, I think that's going to be the best part of the whole day. Unless, naturally, a plane lands on you in the parking lot."

He just looked at me, and I walked away.

"Where's the videographer going?" my mother said as she watched him pack his stuff into his car and drive off.

"He got eighty-sixed," I said. "See, this is the time when it pays off to have bar friends, including bouncers who donated their services in lieu of a present."

"Oh, good," my mother commented. "A drunk bride. How pretty. You're acting like Liza Minelli at your wedding! Where is that bartender? I'm going to sue that moron, I paid him extra to pour you weak drinks!"

If my mother wanted to see a good example of inebriation, all she had to do was look at Jamie. She shot out on the dance floor like a bullet, wineglass in her hand, as soon as the DJ played "Walk This Way."

"I love this song so much," she shouted as she ran, "that it makes me want to quit my job and become a stripper!"

While my mother's friends looked on, dancing in their step-together-step Protestant Accountant dance, Jamie planted her legs firmly apart and whipped her head around like she was putting out a fire with it.

"Just give me a keeeeeessssss," she sang to herself, her eyes closed. "Like this!"

"What is it that she does for a living?" a woman from my father's office asked me from behind a cupped hand.

"She's a microbiologist," I said flatly, not taking my eyes off my best friend's Aerosmith-induced fit. "Cancer research. She'll probably save your life one day."

As soon as the song was over, the DJ announced that it was time for all of the "old maids" to gather on the dance floor, a phrase that did not sit very well with one particularly pickled microbiologist, since she is exactly, to the day, a week older than I am.

She looked at him, pointed her finger with her free hand, staggered several feet, and then shrieked, "Whaddaya mean *old maids,* ha? The term is *unclaimed treasure,* buddy, *unclaimed treasure!*"

Ten minutes later, my mother informed me that the wedding was over. She said that the caterer was tired and wanted to break down the tables and go home.

"And you know, if you get divorced within a year, you owe your father for all the liquor your friends drank," she told me. "Because these people can outdrink the navy! Like the guy that threw up in the fondue pot and that guy over there sleeping under that table. He was the one smoking those horrible-smelling cigarettes! I bet they were French. *Young man, where are your friends?*"

I told the DJ to play one last song. I took my shoes off and sat down at an empty table.

It was over. Done with. Finished.

In a way, I was happy and relieved, but in another way, I couldn't help but wonder what the hell had happened.

The groom and I got our things together and, still wearing our wedding clothes, piled into his Honda, where my dress proceeded to become garnished with grease and car dirt.

We drove to Circle K and got ThirstBusters, and then went home.

We were married.

It Takes Guts

It was gray, steaming, piled high, and smelled like a sewer when the plate was placed in front of my husband.

I looked at him.

He looked at me.

Despite the reflex that urged me to vomit, I smiled. "Looks good," I said from behind my teeth. "Dig in!"

He hesitated for a moment, then picked up his fork and pushed around the contents of his plate.

I was trying very hard to concentrate on my own food, chicken-fried steak, which arrived a second after my husband's. Chicken-fried steak. Tested and true, I live for this stuff. But the smell—or rather stench, shall I call it—wafting over from the other side of the table hit me with the same speed my mother's open-handed slap did a split second after the first time I called my little sister a "buck-toothed retard."

Honestly, I couldn't raise my eyes, I just could not bring myself to do it. I stared at my own meal, cut a piece of steak, and then took the first bite.

I had already sensed trouble long before our lunch reached the table. My husband, friend to all men, embracer of all cultures, had done a stupid, stupid thing. As the waiter at my favorite soul food restaurant was about to take our order, he mentioned that the special that day was chitlins. I passed over that information with a stern grimace, and delivered my choice of chicken-fried steak. My husband then told the waiter that he would like pork chops, and then paused.

"On second thought," he said as he looked off into the distance, "I think I'll have the special."

Now, if my life was a comic strip instead of the senseless repeatings of tragedy and disappointment that it is, the next frame of this scene would illustrate my husband and me sitting at our table, the waiter smiling slightly, and a lighted sign above my husband's head—all in red letters—that read "ONE DUMB HONKY."

Instead, the waiter took on the sly smile and went back to the kitchen.

"Are you crazy?" I shot at my husband. "Chitlins? You ordered chitlins? Do you have any idea what that is?"

"No," my husband admitted. "But I think it might be part of a neck bone."

"I don't," I replied. "I think it's skin. Little chunks of pig skin all fried up and fatty."

"Well, I'm adventurous," my husband continued. "You know I like to experiment with food."

Oh yes, I knew that part quite well. I've seen his examples of food research on numerous occasions, like the time he dumped an entire sleeve of saltine crackers into a glass of milk and produced glue strong enough to hold up drywall; gobbling up Dinty Moore beef stew or chili cold and right out of the can; the regular habit he had during his bachelor days of preparing a box of "economy" mac and cheese by forsaking the milk and butter and simply using water to mix the sauce instead; and another favorite meal of his that consisted of boiling some macaroni until limp, squirting a packet of Taco Bell hot sauce on it, and proclaiming it "mighty good eatin'." All of those occasions, however, were rather innocuous compared with this one. At least during those times, we knew what part of the animal the food came from, and how many months a normal person would have to go without sustenance before he actually considered eating it.

"I bet that you're going to get a plate full of nothing but boiled lips and assholes," I predicted in a whisper, adding, "Cracker!"

I think it's safe to say that the aroma of the chitlins arrived at our table before the vision of it did.

I shot my husband another look, as if to say, "I told you, no more farts in public places," but I was wrong.

Boiled, gray, and piled up real high on that plate was a heaping helping of intestines.

That's what I said.

Guts.

Now, I really don't want to criticize the delicacies of a heritage that isn't my own, but my mother used to make something similar called tripe, and I can say confidently that it looked equally obscene and smelled just as bad as my relatives gobbled it up. As a child, I just stood by, imagined a peaceful place and the wish list of toys I hoped to get on my next birthday in my head, and did the best I could to suppress the impulse to gag.

I put those childhood tools back to work.

"Want a bite?" my husband said as he chewed his first mouthful.

"Honestly," I said without a pause, "I'd rather harvest my own eggs and make an omelette with my toenail clippings than sample your lunch."

After the second bite, my husband said he was full, so we paid the bill and headed home.

Three hours later, as the memory of the chitlin smell was beginning to pass, my husband burped.

"Oh, that was bad," he related as he fanned the stink my way.

I felt my stomach flip.

"Oh," he continued, "God. That's just reminding me how rough it was on one side and kind of slimy on the other."

My stomach did a back flip and nearly dismounted.

"Please," I said as I headed toward the bathroom. Resist, I told my stomach, lie back down. Flowers and grass, I smell flowers and grass and the smell of Bubblegum Bonnie Bell Lip Smackers—

"Jesus! Wooo!" my husband exclaimed. "It was really slimy—"

"I said please stop," I pleaded.

"—and it felt a little chunky as I chewed it . . ."

Even though I was picturing flowers and grass and a Barbie town house fully furnished, it was too late. Way too late. I don't even believe if a Barbie town house had materialized right before my eyes I could have stopped it. It was out of my hands, and I leaned forward and barfed straight into the toilet.

"Looks like that chicken-fried steak didn't agree with you," my husband said as he handed me a damp cloth. "Maybe you should have ordered what I did."

Grin and Bare It

I already know I'm not *Playboy* material. I'm a mess.

Aside from an episode of Forced Nudity while trying on wedding dresses, I haven't been completely and voluntarily naked since I was four, and besides, God didn't intend for me to be a Playmate when he made me. I don't run, I gallop. I don't walk, I trudge. I'll eat lunch and talk to five people afterward before I realize I have refried beans on my cheek. I once flossed my teeth with a strand of my own hair. Each of my hips has more shelf space than my refrigerator and freezer combined.

But there I was, sitting in a villa at the Biltmore Hotel, wrapped in a thick, thirsty white bathrobe with a bunny embroidered on the lapel, filling out an application for the Playboy Playmate contest.

It wasn't really my idea, honest. I was sent to cover the contest for a feature story, and was interviewing the photo editor, Kevin, when I decided to put him on the spot and ask him what he thought my chances were of becoming the centerfold of the new millennium.

"You should try out," he flattered me. "You never know when we'll want to do a spread with reporters and writers!"

"Well, If you pick me, you'll have to pay for my liposuction," I mentioned. "I've got enough lard in just one of these cheeks to make tamales for every man, woman, child, and wild dog in the state of Oaxaca!"

"You should do it," he urged. "How else can you write about what the tryouts are like?"

He's kind of right, I thought, and hell, I'm always up for a humiliating experience that leaves me feeling entirely inadequate and rather hopeless, kind of like coming home from a great date only to discover that on the side of your nose, there's a whitehead the size of a marble.

Surrounding me was a room full of mutants, genetically blessed creatures that had no business calling themselves human, clad in bikinis, high heels, and robes swinging wide open. One of them didn't have a single freckle on her entire body, and another one had what I can only assume were the bones of her pelvis poking out so far they nearly broke her skin. I looked down at my own arm, sprinkled with enough spots and dots to make their own constellation, and thought, Man, the next time someone sees the bones of my pelvis, it will be at my autopsy!

There were so many boobs in that room—I mean, they were everywhere—that the only thing that popped in my head was "Got Milk?" There was one endowed lady who was so . . . bountiful that I couldn't figure out how she even managed to brush her teeth, and that's when I realized I was staring at THEM. At her. I felt like a guy, but I couldn't help it. They were circus big, and defied gravity so devoutly I was positive the implants were reinforced by magnets.

"How many payments do you have left?" I wanted to ask her, but was afraid that she'd hit me with one of them and knock me out cold. So what if my "best feature" touches my lap when I sit down, so what? I reminded myself. At least they don't accrue an annual percentage rate on my Visa.

I took a deep breath and settled down to fill out the application form.

Height, the application requested.

"5'6"," I fudged.

Weight. "N/A," I wrote.

Hair. I thought a moment. "Clean," I jotted. "AND strong enough to dislodge a particularly stubborn piece of corn!"

Special Achievement. "In 1994, I quit smoking," I scribbled, "gained forty pounds, and got a guy to marry me anyway."

I signed the model release just in time for David, the photographer, to tell me that he was ready for me.

"Okay," he said as I entered the bedroom they had set up as a studio, "you can disrobe now."

I untied the robe and stood there.

"Um," he said, looking at me, still covered in my gray jumper, black shirt, and tights. "Didn't you want to . . . change?"

"If I take any of this off," I said kindly, "waves of horror will burn your corneas to a crisp, and you'll probably grab the nearest utensil to claw them out yourself. Really, I'm acting in your best interest."

David nodded. "Okay, well, then, lean on the bed over here and kind of shake your hair with your hands," he instructed me. "Now smile!"

I leaned on the bed, I lifted my arms up to tousle my hair, I smiled. Then I smelled bagels. Onion bagels. "You have snacks in here?" I asked, looking around.

"No," he said as he clicked the first photo. "Turn your head more to the right."

I complied, thinking him stingy not to share until I caught a really strong whiff of a Jewish deli and realized it was coming from my right armpit.

"Well, that's enough of that pose!" I said, shooting my arms straight down to their sides.

David came over and positioned me for the next photo, turning me completely around. "Hold still," he said as he backed away. "Hey, I think lunch is here. I smell onion bagels!"

I stood staring at the wall, and then it hit me. "You're taking a heinie shot!" I cried. "You're shooting my heinie?"

"It's a big lens," he commented. Click. "Okay, we're done. You did VERY WELL."

"You know my mother is going to make me go to confession for this," I said as I handed him back the bathrobe and gathered up my stuff. "But if you choose me for a pictorial of reporters, the only way I'll do it is if you put my nudie shots in between Barbara Walters's and Helen Thomas's."

On my way out, I passed by the girl I had gawked at earlier. I smiled. She smiled slightly, sweeping her eyes over my jumper, and then sneered.

I stopped. "David said I did VERY WELL," I mentioned. "But I think I'll actually score a lot higher on the essay part of the contest."

Her face dropped. "There's an essay?" she said, shocked.

"Oh yeah." I nodded. "With footnotes and everything."

Visibly, her panic grew. "I can't write with my feet!" she cried.

"Better start practicing!" I said with a tiny giggle before I headed out the door.

I Think at Night It Flies

It's 2 A.M., and I'm sitting on my couch in the living room in the dark, wearing only a sweatshirt and my underwear. I have a stuffed, fleece alligator in my right hand, and am shaking it at the growling creature stalking my feet. Neither my husband nor I have had a full night's sleep in a week.

It was completely our fault and we knew it. We bought into the dream, refinancing our patience and sanity to do it. When we spotted the puppy in a wet cage at the pound, she was soaked, crying, and shaking. As she licked our fingers through the wire, her coat dripping and matted, we knew we had to save her and take her home. After she had been spayed the next day, we went to retrieve her, and were presented with a sweet, lolling puppy and the words "Here's your dog. Don't wash her for ten days."

"This is a good dog," my husband said as we watched her sleep that night in her newly prepared wicker bed. We both marveled at how lucky we were to have such a calm, well-dispositioned puppy.

The next morning, however, my husband frantically woke me up. "I think there's something wrong with that dog," he said. "She's showing symptoms I saw in *Old Yeller*. She keeps biting me and growling, I'm about to name her 'Foamy' and take her out to the barn to put her down."

"That's okay," I said, getting out of bed. "She's just coming around, getting used to us. All puppies bite and play."

But when we entered the living room, it looked like a blizzard had struck. "This wasn't here a minute ago," my husband said, picking up a torn, shredded piece of toilet paper from the floor.

"It's my fault," I admitted. "I shouldn't have left the roll on the coffee table."

"Did you leave the Tootsie Rolls from Halloween out, too?" he asked, lifting up his foot, displaying the chocolate prize that had lodged between his toes.

"Do you want me to say yes," I said slowly, "or tell you the truth that we didn't have any left?"

That was when we realized that the puppy wasn't GOOD when we brought her home, she was just SEDATED.

The commercials for Puppy Chow don't show this part of dog babyhood on TV, I learned over the next couple of days. They don't show that after spending forty bucks on puppy toys, her favorite playthings will actually consist of an empty toilet paper roll and a plastic tampon applicator she wrestled out of the box. They don't show the puppy lunging for my ears like Mike Tyson, or her miraculously producing two sounds at the same time, a growl and a primal scream, like a Tibetan monk. They don't show the already existing pets in the house ducking for cover under beds, in closets, and behind bathtubs, fearful that their private parts will be mutilated by puppy teeth, the only part of them she can reach. They don't show that new puppy parents should always wear hiking boots, or face the wrath of those same teeth gnawing at their ankles like a paw stuck in a trap. They don't show that she will try to claw her way to freedom via your recently refinished wood floors, or that you will smell doody everywhere, but won't find it until it's attached to you. They don't show that she doesn't even like Puppy Chow, and prefers to fish her meals out of the deposits left in the kitty box.

I think that someone should have the responsibility of telling you this before you get a new puppy, because people forget. It's been eleven years since the last time I brought a fuzzy creature home, the same creature who is now a graying, chunky old lady that looks at me from behind the pillows on the couch with disgust out of her one good eye.

"How could you have been so stupid?" she seems to be saying to me. "I thought you guys were being 'careful.' I don't know how this happened. I sleep at the foot of the bed and I'm with you ALL THE TIME. Now I've got this dog that wants to nurse on me, and I'm seventy-seven years old! Look at you, you've got a smashed Tootsie Roll stuck to your shoe."

The cat's sentiments were easily as hostile. "I hate you more now than I did yesterday" was the message he sent me. "I'm going to pee on something you just bought!"

They were right. We had lost complete control of our house, relinquished it to a three-pound hairball of terror that caused my husband to speculate aloud, "I think at night . . . IT FLIES."

How were we supposed to know about the dangers? There certainly wasn't a sign posted outside of her cage that read, "This puppy will cost you 742 hours of sleep, six fights with your spouse, the respect of your other pets, $3,000 to repair valuable antiques, and will think for a very long time that 'no-no' means 'Good girl! Do it again!' "

After taking her to the vet and confirming that she was not rabid or an infant grizzly bear left at the pound by mistake, my husband decided to try his own method of reclaiming control.

"GRRRR! GRRRR!" he mimicked as he played with the puppy on the couch.

"I don't think you should do that," I snapped. "You're teaching her to be vicious!"

"Don't pick at your ankle scabs. The smell of fresh blood excites her," he whispered back. "GRRRR! I'm teaching her that I'm in charge. I am the alpha dog!"

The puppy backed down for a minute, rolled onto her back, and grew quiet.

He looked up and smiled. "See?" he said.

"Well, then, I'm not going to bother making dinner," I said. "The cat just had a bowel movement big enough for the both of you."

"GRRRR," he said, lunging for my ankle.

Sweet Ride

The key was gone.

It was GONE.

It had been looped around my finger the second before, and now it had vanished. I was in big, BIG trouble.

The first thing I did was leave my groceries in front of the checkout and I ran as fast as my two-ton legs would carry me.

Oh God, oh God, I kept thinking as I felt my fat, and particularly my two most prominent abdominal tubes, bounce up and down as I gathered all of the energy I had been storing for the past fifteen years precisely for an emergency just like this and RAN.

I ran out of the store like a quarterback, complete with noises. I didn't really care. I just needed to know if I was going to live to see another day.

I ran into the parking lot, stopped short, and skimmed the horizon. Red roof, brown roof, truck roof. BING! Silver roof, black louvers on the back window of the 1984 300ZX, she's safe.

I breathed a sigh of relief. She's safe.

My mother's car was SAFE.

I was already back in the store when I realized that although the car was still there—no one had stolen it—I still couldn't get in it. The key was mysteriously gone. Vanished.

I have nightmares about things like this, stress dreams that cause me to wake up in the middle of the blackness, clawing at my own skin. In these dreams, I have my mom's car, and I have eaten the key. Or I have fed it to my monkey-baby. Or have traded it for a fifteen-year-old Monte Carlo with a chain steering wheel and a barely clothed, abundantly endowed, and lust-absorbed Viking maiden painted on the hood.

It's true. I hate that car.

Haaaaaaaaate it.

When I'm driving that car, I feel as if danger is all around me, ready to give me a big hug. I feel like I'm a target for every driver who didn't make their last insurance payment. I feel like there is no safe place to park it, that as soon as I walk away, the battered door of a 1975 Plymouth will rip through the body of my mother's car like a can of tuna. Every time I pull into my driveway, I pray that my foot correctly hits the brakes and not the gas, because I feel like I'm going to drive the Z right through my kitchen. I feel like a midget because it's so low to the ground, and I basically have to roll out of it. And, worst of all, when I'm driving it, I feel like Stevie Nicks. I constantly find the words "Stand back, stand back," "Chain, keep us together," and "TUSK!" running through my head, and on more than one occasion, I've had to look into the rearview mirror to convince myself that I'm not wearing a gauze dress, or have something tied around my head or silver sprinkly things on my face.

I'm living the horror of the eighties all over again. The car is telling me to get my hair frosted, slap a snake bracelet around my bicep, do some speed, and date a guy with a bilevel.

I feel like that car makes me seventeen again, which is the exact age I was when my mother traded in her Country Squire station wagon and brought the Z home. My boyfriends would drop me off at home after a date, gasp, "Wow, dude, is that your car? The 300? Um, I've changed my mind and you are prettier than Andrea Zakalovas, after all. She only has a 280Z."

I hate the Z.

My car, my little Honda Accord, is broken, and has been in the shop now, as of today, for ten days. When I realized I wasn't getting it back, my parents offered to let me use the Z, and though I protested, though I told them that they'd probably get it back damaged, they gave me the key anyway.

I was distraught on the way home that day, so upset, I had to stop and get a Cherry Limeade at Sonic. I paid the girl with $1.29 in assorted change, and began to count it for her when she stopped me.

"Don't worry," she said. "I trust you."

Who? I thought as she towered five feet above me as I looked up at her basically from the curb. You mean ME?

Then I stopped myself from laughing. Take a good look, a voice inside my head mentioned.

I'm a midget driving a 1984 300ZX, it's got 58,000 miles on it, and K-EZ is the only station the radio will get.

What's not to trust?

What's not to trust. My finger, from which the key to the Z had been hanging, is still empty. I'm mere seconds away from a full-fledged panic. I can't find the key. It's not in my purse, not in either of my pockets, not in my hand.

I've lost it.

I'm going to have to call my dad, call my dad and tell him I've lost the key to the car. I am in so much trouble.

I'm going to get yelled at.

Then I'll get the silent treatment.

Then, I'll get grounded.

I bet he'll ground my husband, too.

Wait!! I have a husband. My dad can't ground me, I have a husband! I don't live at home anymore, and he's too scared of my neighborhood to drive down there and make sure I stay in the house!

Thank God I'm too old to get smacked. I became old enough

last year that it ceased being discipline and is now considered felony assault.

"Ma'am! Ma'am!" I hear a small voice cry from behind me, and then I see it. Looped around the cashier's forefinger is a yellow neon-colored number one, the key to the Z hanging limply from it.

I gasp with relief. "Thank you, thank you, thank you," I repeat over and over to her, as I pull out my own set of keys and hook the one to the Z onto them.

"This chain," I say to her, almost out of breath, "this chain will keep us together!"

Marathon Man

It didn't hit me that he was serious until he brought the box home.

"Look," my husband said, lifting the lid and exposing two matched bright and shiny shoes. "They're new!"

"Those look like running shoes!" I balked.

He took a deep breath and shot me a look. "They *are* running shoes," he said, shaking his head. "I told you I'm going to run that marathon with some people at work. We're a team!"

I never believed him. How could I? We're not running people. We're not even people who walk very fast. We're shufflers. Look at our shoes. It's always the outside rim that gets worn out first. That's more of a mark of Quasimodo than Jesse Owens.

"We're not built for that sort of thing. The most athletic activity we engage ourselves in is chewing," I said, shocked at how much I really did sound like my mother. "Bringing those things into this house is sacrilege!"

The thought of my husband jogging secretly scared me. One of the big reasons I married him was because he wasn't a jock. That was on my list of things to avoid when choosing a spouse. Don't marry anyone who weighs less than you. Don't marry anyone who refers to you as "my old lady," "the Warden," or "babe." Don't marry a guy who drives a Camaro, has cropped hair in front though the back is long, savage, and free, and who ever in his lifetime wore a Warrant T-shirt. Don't marry a guy who would rather burn calories than sit on the couch with me, eating chips and dip. Even the first time my husband watched a basketball game I was horrified and felt betrayed but figured, well, at least he's sitting down. Our relationship is still solid.

"Did you want to borrow a bra?" I said. "Those things hurt when they bounce up and down, you know."

"I'm going to pretend to ignore that last comment because hatred is better than carbohydrates when it comes to fueling an athletic body," he said, lifting his leg up to the arm of the couch and leaning over toward it. "I'm going to take it out on the track!"

"Okay, Marathon Man," I shot. "But you just remember what happened last time you did something sporty!"

I didn't really need to remind him. We're still paying the bills for the ambulance ride and the months of physical therapy he had to endure after hitting a sandbank on a dirt bike last year and dislocating his shoulder. While his brother went for help, my husband lay in the desert for a couple of hours like a pork chop as big, filthy birds started to circle from above. When he finally got to the hospital, they shot him up with morphine, after which he burst into a monologue of Elizabethan verse and scared a couple of nurses who were dressing his arm in a sling. Fortunately, the accident happened in October, so for Halloween, we put a ballpoint pen in my husband's hand and he went as Bob Dole.

I had visions of this marathon ending the same way. I was convinced that he would finish this race on a stretcher after he ran into a light pole or a parked car. I, in turn, would be forced to spend the remainder of the day listening to a soliloquy from *Macbeth* in some emergency room, repeatedly telling him that the damn spot was nothing more than the crust of the Ding Dong I'd dropped in my lap at breakfast.

For a month, my husband trained, stopped indulging in bad

habits, and started eating dried fruit. He had become determined, dedicated to his dream. He had become a runner.

The night before the race, I had a horrible nightmare. I was at
the race, watching the runners, and all of a sudden, loud peals of
laughter broke out from the crowd. As I looked to see what was
causing the commotion, I saw my husband pass, and I gasped. He
was running like a girl. His little arms twirled in circles as they
flailed from his body, and people started to point, calling out,
"Look at the girlie guy! Hey, Pansy Man, are you running or making meringue?"

I was just waking up from this dream when I smelled something
foul, and noticed my husband sitting on the edge of the bed. Next
to him was a little jar of Icy Hot, and he was generously smearing
it on every part of his body that bends.

"You smell like a rest home," I said. "If you insist on putting
that in your hair, there's nothing I can do to help you."

"Take it out on the track!" I heard him say to himself as he
walked out of the room. "Take it out on the track!"

"When you run, Forrest, run," I called out after him, "do me a
favor and keep your hands down at your sides! Think of manly
things, like chopping down trees or building fires, and don't even
picture a lemon meringue pie!"

When the rest of his team arrived at our house, they pinned
their numbers on and did some last-minute stretching.

I saw him as he pointed to two overflowing ashtrays on the coffee table and showed them to the team. "This is Laurie's, and this
is the Warden's, too," he continued, picking up my inhaler. I scurried back into the hallway before I was forced to listen to the
healthy people giggle.

An hour later, I was at the ballpark, standing with the rest of the
people watching the runners cross the finish line. I was afraid that
I had gotten there late, but after I saw that the runners who were
finishing were still in fairly good physical condition, I was sure
I hadn't missed my husband. I stood for a while as the crowd

cheered them on, and suddenly, I smelled old people and then I saw him.

He jogged right past me, thin streams of sweat running down his face, his eyes staring straight ahead. He wasn't even bleeding, though there were little bits of grass and a candy wrapper stuck to one of the Icy Hot spots. No one was laughing, his arms were bent at the proper angles, and by some divine miracle, his shorts hadn't risen up between his thighs.

He had done it.

I jumped and waved and heard myself scream, "Yea, honey!" and inside my heart, I felt a little flutter, but I don't think it was a heart attack from physically exerting myself.

I think that, maybe, it was pride.

My Poor Sister

My sister and her husband decided one day that they wanted a baby.

"Are you sure?" I asked her. "They're a lot of work and your nipples will get as big as hubcaps."

"They will not," she answered. "We're going to start trying right away."

Six days later, she called me again.

"Guess what?" she said. "I'm pregnant."

"Are you sure?" I asked. "Maybe you just ate something that was dead too long."

"No, it's true," she assured me. "The pink dot says so."

"It's impossible," I said. "Take another test."

"I've taken seven," she asserted. "Seven pink dots say you're going to be an aunt."

"What did you do?" I asked her. "Put your ovaries underneath your pillow last night and wait for a visit from the Fertility Fairy?"

This was weird. How could my baby sister have a baby? And how was she going to tell my parents? I knew damn well that it didn't matter that she had been married for over a year; they were still going to try and ground her.

But I guess they took it okay, despite the fact that my mother wanted a signed and notarized note from the doctor to prove it, and my dad didn't get violent or anything. He just looked my brother-in-law in the eye starkly and said, "I wasn't aware that you did that sort of thing."

They were going to be grandparents. I was going to be an aunt.

My sister and her husband were excited. They started looking at cribs and strollers and decided which room would be the nursery. They bought the baby its first toy, a teddy bear that played "You Are My Sunshine" when you wound it up.

I caught my sister lying on the couch in her house one day with the wound-up bear on her stomach.

"What are you doing?" I asked.

"I'm playing the song so the baby can hear it," she said with a smile.

"I hate to be the buzzkill," I said honestly, "but the baby still has a tail. It could still be a fish. It doesn't have ears, and it's got the thought process of a ballpoint pen."

She didn't listen to me, and kept the bear right in its place on her stomach.

She started to get big. And got bigger. And bigger. And BIGGER. By her seventh month, I was ecstatic because I wasn't the fattest person in my wedding party anymore. She lost her belly button and instead got a big, brown circle on her stomach and her breasts each weighed as much as a four-door Lexus.

If you looked closely at her midsection, you could see the baby—which by now had become a mammal and was in the shape of a boy—squirming around like an alien. Her feet were so swollen that she couldn't wear regular shoes, so she took to wearing foot apparel from Kmart that looked like a lace-up cast.

"Just so you know, you're wrong," my sister informed me. "My nipples are not the size of hubcaps. They more proportionately resemble dinner plates."

My poor sister. I was starting to feel really, really sorry for her, especially when she started that swayback waddling thing because if she stood up straight, she'd topple right over.

"What if he's ugly and we don't know it?" she said to me one day. "What if we think he's the most beautiful baby and he really looks like Ernest Borgnine? How will we know?"

"Pictures," I said after I thought for a while. "That's how. Pictures can't lie. And if I detect ugliness, I will tell you, I swear. I won't let you have an ugly baby without knowing it."

That night, I had a dream in which the baby was born with teeth growing out of his nose and my sister kept insisting that it was normal.

"It's totally okay," she said repeatedly. "You've never had a baby, so how would you know? We just have to use a different kind of toothbrush."

From that night on, the vision of nose teeth haunted me, and I hoped with everything I had that the baby would not be born a javelina.

The morning that my sister's water broke it was early and her husband asked her if she had wet the bed. She called me right away, and I told her I'd meet her at the hospital, and I rushed as fast as I could. When I got there, she was hooked up to some monitor thing that measured her pain as the contractions gripped her belly. She was starting to go off the chart.

It looked awful. We weren't allowed to talk when the numbers on the monitor were rising, and if we did, she would get a look on her face like a wild animal ready to bite your leg off. After she was forced by her pain to mutter the F word a couple of times, she made us leave, and after several hours, his head popped out, then his shoulders, and we all had a brand-new baby.

He was fat, he was purple, and he had two black eyes, but he was perfect. He stuck his hand in his mouth right away and that's when we knew he was a genius baby.

He was Prince Nicholas, and after I checked for any signs of dental work in his nostrils, he was the most beautiful baby I had ever seen.

Following Instructions

The bead of sweat ran down the length of my nose, paused silently on the very, very, very tip before it rolled suddenly forward, leapt, and careened toward the floor, flattening when it hit.

"I CAN follow directions! I built THAT!" I yelled, pointing to a bookcase on the far side of the room.

"I refinished and reassembled THOSE!" I bellowed, pointing to the mantel of my fireplace and the two flanking glass-fronted cabinets.

"I GOT AN ELECTRIC MITER SAW FOR MY BIRTHDAY," I roared at the ceiling, my arms open wide, "AND A CHAIN SAW FOR CHRISTMAS!"

Surely, I was indeed qualified for the task at hand. It shouldn't have been any trouble at all for me to assemble the two-shelf cabinet that I had just hauled into my living room from the home improvement store. My troubles began after I poised the seventy-pound box against the wall and sliced it open with a utility knife, only to discover that both the instructions and the hardware were MIA. To remedy the problem, I called the store to inform them of the situation, and to inquire if they could locate another set for me.

The first fellow I talked to listened patiently, then put me on hold to conduct a reconnaissance hardware mission. Moments later, another fellow, Daniel, picked up the line and asked if he could help me.

"Thank you, but I'm already being helped," I replied.

"Obviously NOT," he snapped at me. "If you were, they'd be on the phone RIGHT NOW."

Who am I to judge the wisdom and expertise of a warehouse worker? Clearly, I knew not of which I spoke, being a mere amateur in the world of home improvement customer service. So I repeated my story again.

"We don't have any of those cabinets left," Daniel informed me simply.

"Can you . . . check?" I brazenly ventured.

"I don't need to CHECK," he said. "I KNOW."

"Well, there was a whole stack of them there two hours ago."

Daniel took a deep breath. "YOU KNOW," he said in his best spouse-abuser voice, "I'm standing IN FRONT of the cabinets right now and they're all gone, but I guess *you know best*. They must all be invisible to ME!"

What could I do now? I bit my nail, and looked at the box in my living room filled with useless wooden planks. Then I got my keys.

When I got to the home improvement store, I slipped down the cabinet aisle, found the box I needed, and, well, helped myself to the parts that were missing from my box and wrote, "This Box is Incomplete and Invisible: See Daniel," on the top. Then I ran out of the store as fast as I could without further aggravating the inner-thigh burn I had acquired the week before at the gym.

Back at home, I got my screwdriver and went to work. With the illustration-only instructions in hand, I assembled the frame of the cabinet according to the pictures, even though I was missing the part that looked like a gumdrop and used the part that looked like a Chiclet instead.

I stepped away from the cabinet and looked at it. Then I did a bad thing. With the brush of one fingertip, it was reduced to a pile

of laminated chipboard that scared my little dog so badly she tinkled on the floor.

I noticed the first bead of sweat streaming down my forehead
when I saw the toll-free number at the bottom of the booklet, and
the words FOR HELP CALL next to it.

"Hi, this is Melissa, how can I help you?"

"Tragically, Melissa," I began, "I have just purchased three
hundred dollars of your merchandise [a gross exaggeration, but
necessary for impact] and I'm returning it ALL. I have never seen
such poor quality."

"You certainly have the right to do that," she replied.

That wasn't the answer I thought I'd get, since I was looking for
something more along the lines of "I am so, so sorry"; "Oh no!
Please don't! Please!" or some gulping, audible sobs.

"I have tools," I stammered. "So I know poor quality when I see
it!"

"Okay," she answered before she disconnected me.

I stared at the phone, then at the heap of cabinet. I was more
determined than ever to put it together. For the next two hours, I
wrestled, wrangled, and fought with the planks, studying the instructions, and following them step by step. I didn't touch the finished product this time. It fell apart when the oscillating fan
turned toward it.

"Hi, this is Sandy, how can I help you?"

"Sandy," I began, "can you explain to me why—after I have
spent seven hundred dollars on your products—they have such a
problem getting along with *gravity?*"

"Oh, sorry," Sandy replied, and that's when I thought we were
finally getting somewhere. "Gravity doesn't come with the cabinets. It's an accessory that's purchased separately! Would you like
a list of stores that carry it?"

I looked back at the pile. Then I kicked it. A plank flew across
the floor and put a gaping, fresh dent in the bookcase I had built.

I picked up the instructions and looked at them again. On the very last page, next to a diagram of what should have been my newly assembled cabinet, it said, "You will need:" and showed a picture of a drill, then the words *"Quizas necesite ayuda,"* which, with the help of my Spanish dictionary, meant "An assistant may be helpful."

"Hi, this is Denise, how can I help you?"

"Denise," I said wearily, my voice cracking, "who's writing these instructions? My drunk uncle Rossie? Is he being helped by my cousin Ray-Ray with the one eye that always stays looking at his nose?"

"No, I don't think so," Denise said, pausing for a moment. "I think his name is Bill. Yes. I'm pretty sure it was Bill."

"Can you leave BILL a message for me?" I continued. "Can you ask him why—after I've spent two thousand dollars and nine hours trying to assemble your merchandise—why he failed to mention that I'd need a drill until the very last page? Could you also tell him that you'll also need some superglue, staples, and a bunch of rope, though I'm saving a bit of that to hang myself with. Oh, and one more thing, tell him this, too: NOT TOO MANY PEOPLE I KNOW HAVE A SPANISH-SPEAKING ASSISTANT!!!"

"Would you like me to send you a set of instructions on how to assemble one?" Denise asked.

The M&M, the Bee,
and the Man Baby

After my little sister had her baby, things really changed in my family.

My father, who made my sisters and me drive cars all during high school that he was going to "restore" when he retired, bought a brand-new Toyota minivan for my five-day-old nephew because his car seat didn't fit well enough in the back of my sister's unrestored car.

My mother, whose only hobbies were smoking and ordering useless appliances from QVC, kicked the nicotine habit, changed the channel to public television, and added an extra *ie* syllable after nearly every word, as in "bott-ie," "blank-ie," and the ever-popular "diap-ie."

I, the one who swore she would talk to him as an adult and not talk down to him in that baby voice, have developed a full-blown falsetto, ventriloquist kind of thing because Nicholas does not respond to anything else.

And Halloween took on greater significance than any of us had ever thought possible. While we had come together to decide that we would steer Nicholas away from the White Trash Baby Syndrome by keeping him fully clothed in public places, never have his birthday party at Chuck E. Cheese, and promised that he would never know the taste of a Little Debbie (although my mother came dangerously close to destroying the entire project by buying him a "Who Needs Lotto? I Have Grandma" T-shirt), a river of strife had risen between certain members of the clan, namely my sister and me.

I wanted Nicholas to be a bee for Halloween.

My sister wanted him to be an M&M.

"He'll look stupid as an M&M," I pouted. "If you make him into a brown peanut one, people will think he's a potato. Years from now, he'll look at photographs and inquire why, on the occasion of his first Halloween, we dressed him as a starch."

"The bee is on back order," my sister reminded me. "And he'll look cute as a blue M&M."

"The blue M&M is a poseur," I snickered. "Besides, we don't even know if Nicholas is cute or not."

"Do you think he's cute?" my sister asked me with a wince.

"Yeah," I replied, following up on a promise I had made my sister when Nicholas still lived in his own carrying case.

"But what if he's ugly and we don't know it?" she insisted.

"That would make us look real stupid," I answered, because we knew some people with these babies that looked like they were bred for sideshow purposes and their parents had no idea. And I understood why. He was the closest thing I'd ever have to my own kid, so he had to be cute. There was no alternative, although there was always doubt.

When I saw Nicholas's last round of portraits, I carelessly mentioned that he looked like a Man Baby with a man's head on a little baby body. It didn't look like him at all, I added, but that wasn't enough for my sister not to revoke my godmotherhood.

"The angle of the camera is bad," I tried to explain, but that wasn't enough for my sister not to throw my car keys at me and open the door.

"But Sam Donaldson is NOT a bad-looking guy," I protested. "At least I didn't say Woody Allen or Willard Scott!"

"Sam Donaldson sure would make an ugly bee!" she said as she slammed the door.

She didn't talk to me for two days, and we didn't patch things up until I agreed to baby-sit for her. I would have done anything to get back in the loop.

Secretly, though, I was scared. The only people I had baby-sat in the past ten years were very drunk men. There were some similarities, however, I thought to myself: Nicholas falls asleep in a sitting position, drools consistently, throws up on himself and others, always needs to be held up, makes absolutely no sense when he speaks, and wets himself while clothed. The only quality he didn't possess was the ability to make sexual advances. Clearly, I had the upper hand.

Sure. For about two seconds. The moment I walked through that door on Saturday, he looked at me and then screamed so intensely he didn't even make a sound. The kid didn't breathe for a long time, and finally my sister had to hit him on the back to knock some air into his lungs.

When I tried to change him, he peed on my cheek, and when I burped him, a tunnel of formula shot out of his mouth and into my lap, drenching me. Then he cried, and he drooled, and he pooped all over his leg, and then he cried some more. After forty-five minutes, I was exhausted, frustrated, and ready to cry myself. I tried to take a nap but he kept waking me up. I couldn't wait for my sister and her husband to get home.

When I finally heard their car pull up into the driveway, I was as excited as if my dad had bought me a new van. I waited at the door with the dogs.

"How'd it go?" my sister said as she opened the door.

"He peed on me," I said.

"He does that." She nodded.

"He threw up on me," I said.

"He does that, too." She nodded.

"I got his poop on my hand," I said, holding it out. She nodded.

"He does this to you every day, doesn't he?" I asked. She nodded.

"I think he'd be a cute M&M," I said. "After all, who doesn't love carbohydrates?"

Burning the Bra

I had never been to the outlet mall before.

I had heard about its wonders and the majesty that was held within it; I had listened to others describe the magic of its stores, and how they obtained their dreams almost for free. You could buy, I was told, Wonderbras for three bucks.

Looking at my own bras (a sad collection that predated New Wave), I knew I needed to be a part of it. It called to me.

So then I called my sister, still on maternity leave, and talked her into driving me out to Casa Grande, a literal Mecca of outlet shopping.

Visions of all sorts popped into my head during the drive down there. I was going to get shoes. I was going to buy sheets. I was going to find some great dresses. Casa Grande is a dusty, grimy little colony of waddling diabetics. I was gonna get new bras.

There is something about getting new bras that men will never understand. Never. There's just a quality about wearing a bra in which the underwire is still in its rightful place and hasn't yet caused any bloodshed. There's just something about a clean, unstretched-out strap that lays perfectly flat and isn't covered with nubbies. There's something pristine about a new, flawless cup in which none of the nipple is visible through a tear or hole.

I had even gone up a size, I suspected, although this was due more to an increase in back fat than anything else. This also makes getting bras exciting. It makes you feel like you have more to offer. When we reached the mall, I made my sister head straight for the bra store. She, on the other hand, wasn't as excited as I was. Since she had given birth, things had, well, changed for her.

"There's nothing in this store that could give me enough support. I'm going to have to start tying them up with ropes," she mentioned as we passed through the doors.

It was true. I had never experienced true-life grisly horror before the day she called me a week after she had given birth and insisted that I rush over to her house. I found her sitting on the couch, topless, with a massive suction cup affixed to each breast and tears streaming down her face as she sobbed heavily. She looked like a hybrid of Barbarella and a Holstein in the middle of a shift. It was the stuff of pure science fiction, a bad Star Trek episode/commercial from the Dairy Council. My brother-in-law just stood there, shaking his head as he continually shrugged, until I finally took control of the situation, flipped off the switch to the pump, and said to my sister, "Let me introduce you to your new best friend, Infamil.

"We are a bottle-fed breed, my dear," I told her. "How could you not know that? We're Catholic! Boobs stay covered! Do you think Mary flashed around her bazongas every time her baby cried? Even Jesus was raised on a bottle and a mix! Look at you, trying to be all modern!"

At the bra outlet, I dug through the $2.99 bins, but I only found sizes that I wore when I began to blossom in fourth grade. I was going to have to graduate to the $5.99 racks, which I saw were bursting with bright silks, satins, and knits in all colors of the rainbow. I finally decided on two, plopped down my thirteen bucks, and I had the bras that would see me through my thirties and possibly to menopause. I doubted that a better deal could have been found.

I wanted to put them on right away, though I managed to resist my urges in the car and waited until I got home.

Although I knew that in the bras I was going to more closely resemble Rosie O'Donnell's Secret than Victoria's, they still made me feel good. My right boob didn't pop out of its cup all the time like it did with my other bra, and all of the back hooks were still intact.

I wore one the next day to work, feeling pert, perky, and maybe even a little bit thinner. I felt clean. I also felt a little ticklish.

By noon the little tickle had turned into something of an itch, and by midafternoon, I couldn't keep my hand out from underneath my shirt. My boobs were driving me crazy, and I couldn't get the itching to stop. I would scratch for a second, it would be fine, and then the sensation of a million ants running across what made me a woman was nearly forcing me to scream. It was intolerable.

By the time I ran to my car, the evil apparatus was unhooked and being threaded through my sleeve. I threw the bra in the passenger seat, relieved but still itching. When I got home, I saw the damage: two bright red smiles underneath each boob and two bright red frowns on each. Complete with hives.

My husband was mortified. "What did you do?" he asked in a panic. "Did you try to wax up there?"

"No," I said, wincing. "It's one of the new bras. It gave me bra burn."

Bra burn on a girl with back fat is the furthest thing from attractive, so I decided to go to my mother's to retrieve some aloe vera from her backyard. The minute she saw me, she looked at me funny and exclaimed, "What in the hell is wrong with you? Why are you touching yourself like that? That's a sin, you know."

"I bought a bad bra," I explained. "It burned me."

"There's no such thing as a bad bra," she informed me. "You're probably allergic to something on it. Where did you buy it?"

"The outlet mall." I sighed. "It was five ninety-nine."

"Oh. Well, there you have it. You bought a bad bra. What do you expect for six dollars, a bra that won't make you break out in hives? Who the hell knows who owned that bra before you? Could you not do that in front of me, please?"

For the rest of the night, I had to lie on my bed, with yellow, smelly, sticky, runny aloe vera stuff smeared all over me, topless. Nothing could touch me, otherwise it would itch so bad I would have to scratch it, and I had already begun to make myself bleed. I had scabs. I had hives. I had back fat.

Oh well, I thought as I lay there, the yellow stuff dripping onto my sheets. It could have been worse.

I could have bought underwear, too.

The Lonely, Brown House

They say it's a natural progression. It's an obvious thing, an occurrence that happens to everyone who's recently gotten married.

In fact, I believe legislation has passed in several states that freshly married couples have up to one full year to either A) buy a house or B) have a baby.

If you negligently pass on either obligation, every citizen within the continental United States is fully within their rights to consistently and repeatedly harass and interrogate you about when you will meet your deadline on choice B.

There was no way my husband and I were going to have a baby. We have a dog that I forget to feed at least three times a week, and that doesn't even require unbuttoning my shirt.

What choice did we have? Instead of finding an obstetrician, I called a Realtor and embarked on a trail that would have made Lewis and Clark cringe.

I knew what kind of house I wanted; growing up in the stuccoed, Mexican-tiled, saguaro-landscaped suburbs of Phoenix, I wanted something different. I wanted brick, I wanted a fireplace, and I wanted wood floors. I wanted something interesting with character, history, and a claw-foot bathtub.

I wanted something old.

I was up for a challenge, and determined to find the right house in the right price range. We could commit some elbow grease and sweat equity as long as my potential new neighbors weren't constructing a crystal meth lab in their rompus room or housing eighty illegals. I scanned the newspaper every Sunday, collected real estate magazines, and drove up and down prospective streets with such frequency that parents began to keep their kids inside.

Prospect #1 was a beautiful wood-shingled Tudor Revival with a sweeping lawn and three bedrooms. The minute I stepped in the door, a Leggo whizzed by my head and another struck me in the neck. "Get out! Get out!" screamed the resident children, who were crouched behind the sofa. "You can't have our house! You can't have it!" Their parents, who were outside washing their car, just looked in and grinned. I was puzzled until our Realtor discovered that the house was entering foreclosure, and we quickly left before the children armed themselves with kiddie stun guns or Chinese stars.

Prospect #2 led us to believe that it was an English-style cottage from the exterior. Once inside, however, we knew better. Steeped in that pitiful gold-shag decade we knew as the seventies, the house had not survived a remodeling attempt that included slump block, an overzealous amount of corkboard, and, the coup de grâce, gold-veined mirrors. It looked like Huggy Bear had left only the day before, leaving the water stains from his waterbed permanently soaked into the floor.

Prospect #3 was snatched out from underneath us by an investor with cold, hard cash who planned to gut the Craftsman-style bungalow and "make it modern, you know, with a conversation pit, Berber carpet, and track lighting." Prospects #4, #5, and #6 also fell to the same end, and Prospect #7 inadvertently caught on fire.

After four months of searching, I was beginning to question our luck. Where was the house of our dreams? We had been patient, diligent, giving up our weekends in an effort to homestead. We didn't have large amounts of capital to wage war with investors who proudly exhibited the traits of hyenas, and fixer-uppers were the only homes that fell within our price range. Worse yet, the search was taking a toll on our newborn marriage. Being confined to a car while staking out the downtown neighborhoods in hopes of spotting a "For Sale" sign had spurred such arguments as "The Smell of Your Deodorant Makes Me Nauseous," "Don't Drive Like That With Me in the Car," and the tightrope walker, "If You Would Get a Better Job, We Could Afford It."

We were thrashing in the throes of "That Is Not What I Said to Your Mother" when we drove by it.

"STOP!" I said, throwing my hands up into the air after I spotted the sign in the corner of the yard. "BACK UP! Look . . ."

It was lonely.

It was empty.

It was brown.

"Let's look at it," I said quietly.

It was a little brick bungalow with large windows, a porch, and a big dirt yard.

"Wow," my husband said as he got out of the car. "I like it."

Peeking in the wavy glass of the windows, we saw a fireplace. Wood floors. High, coved ceilings. We strolled along to the back of the house, peeking in every window on the way.

It was my husband who summoned me over, peeking in the bathroom window.

"Come look at this," he said, moving the cobwebs aside.

And there, I saw it. A big, white, cast-iron bathtub with claw feet.

"I want this house," I said as I turned to him. "I want it bad."

"Me, too," he said, and we smiled.

We had found our home.

When we told our Realtor, she arranged for us to take a peek inside the house the next day, and with heels echoing off the wood floors, we toured each room and decided that it was the one.

"It sure has charm," she said with a smile. "Sure is a lot of room here."

We nodded.

"For when that new baby comes," she added with a sly grin.

Erica's Moving Adventure

I had lived in that house for ten years, a third of my life.

When the moving van pulled into my driveway on a Saturday morning, I suddenly realized that I was moving. Although we had bought our new house in September, spent four months restoring it, and had packed a hundred boxes, I was so busy with details I hadn't actually considered that I was leaving. I was too wrapped up with the Disasters of the Week that struck the new house on a regular basis—the faucet of the kitchen sink flying off the wall the moment the water was turned on, the termites that were eating their way through the trees in the front yard, and the lead paint that was flaking off doorjambs and windows in chunks the size of potato chips.

I turned around and the rooms of the old house were empty, save for a mountain of dog hair in one corner, a crumpled piece of newspaper in another. The archaeological layers of my bedroom were unearthed, exposing forgotten Laurie eras. Remnants and pieces of the Lonely, Dramatic, and Drunk Phase were evident in the empty Tylenol PM and whiskey bottles, accented with a million ground-out cigarette butts; the I'll Eat My Way to Happiness Phase revealed bags of Funyons, licorice, and Hershey's chocolate chips, coupled with a vagrant's fortune in empty Pepsi cans; and the Bad Boyfriend Phase dug up torn photographs, charred

letters, and a lock or two of hair, used strictly for black magic purposes.

What was even more frightening than that was the refrigerator.
With the recycling gods frowning on me, I threw away a household's worth of Tupperware and unidentifiable containers, along
with their mysterious contents. Although I had several tubs of
Stroganoff, fajitas, and Chinese food that had most likely grown
into cures for most of the world's deadly diseases, I tossed them
into the trash, where their destiny would now be in the hands of a
city garbage collector.

My husband was busy shoveling all of the crap I had accumu-
lated over the last decade into the U-Haul, which had apparently
seen some scary things itself. One side of the van had been swiped
clean of paint on its back half, leaving the company's motto of
"America's Moving Adventure" into the crippled "erica's Moving
Adventure," and a decapitated saguaro cactus. The sight had
caused several neighbors to cross the street and investigate, asking plainly if I had been indicted for something and was therefore
leaving the country. When we answered that we were only moving,
their next response was to ask us if it would be okay to take all of
the wrought-iron security bars off of my house and put it on their
houses.

Now, the fridge was almost empty except for the containers
that had grown teeth, the sedimentary layers had been cleaned
up, and the trash taken out. I looked around. This house only the
night before had been a home, and served as a storage locker for
memories that I could barely remember and a bunch of things I'd
rather forget.

The day I had moved into the house, my head had swelled up
the night before in an allergic reaction to black hair dye that was
slowly poisoning my blood. My head was so big that my glasses
wouldn't fit around it, and it hurt to hold it up. After I returned to
the new house from the hospital, where I received a massive shot
of steroids in the rear end, I got a phone call from my then-

boyfriend, who informed me that not only had he gotten into a car accident with the U-Haul, but he was in jail. Again. When an officer of the law came to make a report on the accident, an outstanding warrant had been discovered, and the then-boyfriend asked me if I could borrow $10,000 from my parents to pay his bond.

I was just completing this sentimental memory when my husband came into the house, his hands on his hips and a very stern look on his face.

"We can't fit everything in the truck," he said sharply. "You have to decide what stays. We can't take everything. You are definitely going to have to change your lifestyle in the new house."

I hate it when people tell me I have too much stuff.

"We're not on the Oregon Trail, Captain Donner," I snapped back. "It's not like we're going to have to start dumping china closets and beds on the side of the Squaw Peak Parkway because the oxen are too tired to pull the wagon. Fit what you can and we'll come back for the rest."

"THAT'S NOT THE POINT," he said excitedly. "YOU HAVE TOO MUCH STUFF. HOW CAN ONE PERSON HAVE THIS MUCH STUFF? My great-grandparents pushed a handcart across America when they moved. They didn't need this much stuff!"

"You're hungry, aren't you?" I asked quickly.

"Yes, I am!" he answered back.

"Well, because you've done such a good job," I said sweetly, "I've left some really good leftovers in the refrigerator for you."

The Squatter

When a friend announced that she had decided to buy an older home in central Phoenix, I was happy for her.

"It's a great house," she added, "but it's a little dated. The kitchen needs some polish, the floor in the dining room needs to be replaced, and I'm going to have the paneling in the living room removed. I'll have to hire someone. But it's just a little work, I don't think it will take more than a couple of weeks."

"Uh-huh," I replied a little too quickly. "I have just one thing to say to you: Hire a therapist before you talk to anyone who even owns a hammer. I don't want to scare you, but it would be easier to give birth to seven or eight babies at once. If you do that, you automatically get a five-bedroom house in Iowa for free from Oprah. Don't call a contractor. Call a sperm bank."

I almost wished I had. When my husband and I purchased the lonely brown house not far from my friend's, it was our perfect little dream house. Admittedly, we knew it needed a new coat of paint and the bathroom required some updating, but it was just a little work. It shouldn't have taken more than a couple of weeks. Really.

But when I started calling around, I found it wasn't as easy as I thought. One contractor stood in the bathroom, his foot on the rim of the bathtub, snapping his suspenders with his thumbs.

"Well, you see here," he said, tapping on the pipes under the sink with a wrench, "what you've got is galvanized switch-backed back-flow corrosion leading into the alterior ventricle. You're lookin' at a quadruple septic bypass, and I need two thousand dollars up front before I even take my first bite into this monster."

"Wow," I said, stunned. "All that for a new faucet?"

"At least," he nodded, with a snap.

Another contractor informed me that he would need one hundred dollars in cash when he walked through the front door, before he decided if he would even take on the job.

"You want a retainer?" I snapped. "I'm not on trial! My toilet just won't stop running!"

Finally, on the suggestion of some friends, I called Paul, a contractor who had done some plumbing and drywall work for them. On the phone, he was nice, cheery, and said he would meet me at the house after work.

I imagined him driving up in his truck, and out would step a dead ringer for Norm Abrams, the lovable, expert carpenter from *This Old House*. In years to come, I envisioned, Paul would stop by the homestead on Christmas Day armed with a fruit basket and roam around the house to make sure that all of his repairs were still working properly. We'd laugh about the good old days of restoring my house, recounting tender vignettes and drinking brandy in front of the blazing fireplace.

When his truck pulled up, I won't lie that I was a little disappointed when the ninety-eight-pound, red-headed, longhaired man got out, wearing very tight nylon running shorts. Norm would never wear that. We should, he confirmed as he walked around the house, be able to move in in less than a month. It was just a little work. Shouldn't take more than a couple of weeks, he said, really.

He arrived to start working with his partner in tow, a man named Len, who had occasional teeth. Sometimes he had teeth, and sometimes he didn't. You just never knew until he showed up and saliva began shooting out of his mouth like antiaircraft fire.

Replacing the faucet in the bathroom did indeed result in repip-

ing the entire house, a chore that Len fortunately finished before
he was hauled off to the Tent City jail for being a deadbeat dad.
Because of Len's absence, Paul began spending more time at the
house, sometimes working so hard that he just fell asleep there.

Despite the time he was putting in, however, little was getting
done. In fact, weeks would go by when any noticeable work was
finished. "You've got some problems in the attic," Paul explained.
"I have to work on that before I can replace the floor in the bathroom or patch up that broken gas hose in the kitchen. On the safe
side, just keep a window open."

Soon, Paul was in the house all of the time. Sometimes we
would find him sleeping, eating pizza out of a box, or talking on
his cell phone. Rarely, however, did we find him working. When I
saw his truck parked in the backyard with a tarp thrown over it, I
began to have questions.

"Oh, that's nothing, just fell a little behind in my payments," he
said, laughing.

"Did you fall behind in your rent, too?" I asked. "Because I
found your deodorant and a toothbrush in a Baggie in the toilet
tank. You got mail here yesterday. By my calculations, you've been
here for four months."

That was when Paul started to cry. Standing in my laundry
room, he leaned on the dryer he hadn't hooked up yet and began
to wail.

"Len is trying to kill me," he said between sobs. "He's put a
hit out on me from Tent City because I couldn't pay him and he
couldn't make his child support payments. The bank is trying to
repossess my truck, I got evicted from my apartment, and a prose-
cutor is after me because I don't have a contractor's license!"

My blood turned cold. "You mean my house is a hideout?" I
asked.

"If I finished the work," he replied, his head now in his hands,
"I didn't have no place else to go!" Then he ran out of the laundry
room, ripped the tarp off of his truck, and drove away into the
night.

That was the last time I saw Paul, although I got a bill from him several weeks later for work he hadn't even started on yet. Sometimes I wonder where he is now, and if it was the law or Len that caught up to him first.

I do know one thing, and that's if Paul ever stops by to visit on Christmas and talk about the good old days in front of the fire, he'll have to finish the bathroom floor before he gets one sip of brandy.

A Pound of Flesh

On April 14 of last year, I passed a "tax assistance center" on my way to get a Subway sandwich in a strip mall. Through the huge, clear panes of window glass, I saw the horrible vision of a world in limbo. Patrons sat in chairs against the walls, waiting for their turn at assault, their jowls drooping, their shoulders hunched as they clutched their flimsy W-4s as the clock ticked, ticked, ticked. The ones already being helped weren't in any better condition; the life had been sucked out of their features, the vibrancy washed from their skin, and a thin film of perspiration covered their entire bodies. They sat quietly, watching dust float through the air with dead eyes. The tax "helpers" weren't a much improved lot, looking as if they had been recruited from the bus terminal the night before, their qualifications confirmed when it was proven they could count to ten and had, combining both left and right hands, a minimum of five fingers. No one made a sound. Somewhere, quietly, I heard the floating notes from the sound track of *Schindler's List*.

As I walked into Subway, I realized that my appetite was gone, although, honestly, it wasn't helped much when I saw the acne-afflicted Subway teen scratch at his crotch and then manhandle a wheat roll. Gloves, I reminded myself, are no substitute for radiation, and as I left the scene, I passed by the tax assistance center once more, as paramedics tried to revive a man who had foolishly chosen 10 percent withholding, while a little girl in a red coat looked on.

Sometimes you have to learn the hard way.

My accountant, Lee, has seen me at my ugliest, even more so than my gynecologist. He's done my taxes for the last decade, and did them for the first year my husband and I were married. As a newly responsible married person, I proudly presented my very organized stack of tax records to him, and he punched away on his calculator until he suddenly stopped. He explained slowly that now that I was married and filing jointly, it would be a wise idea for my husband and me to consult each other about how many allowances we each took, since combined, it appeared as if we were supporting a small Mormon settlement.

And the government wouldn't believe that, he added.

I laughed about it, mentioned my two dogs and my cat and the fact that we "had a lot of hungry friends," but Lee didn't laugh back. Taxes were serious stuff. He went back to punching in numbers on the calculator and when he finished, he looked up again.

"Twenty-five hundred dollars is what I come up with," he said.

"Wow," I said in amazement. "That's what being married does for you, huh? I had no idea! I would have gotten married before we had sex if I knew it would save us that much!"

"That's not a return," he said, looking at me. "That's what you owe."

I gasped. "But what about my deductions?" I cried.

"Well, surprisingly," he said, "a book of stamps and a pack of paper didn't carry you too far."

"Wait!" I said, flipping through my wallet to find a receipt. "I bought pens, too!"

"From now on," he advised me, "don't count your dogs, the birds that peck at your grass, your cat, any imaginary friends, split personalities, alter egos, or insects that reside inside your house as dependents."

I couldn't help it. I cried. Just put my head in my hands and cried. No doubt Lee had seen this sort of tax behavior before from a new bride who was just too shell-shocked to be humiliated, but he looked away just the same.

It was that day when I found out how easy it is to get in big trouble with the IRS.

Going to jail for tax evasion is probably the stupidest thing in the world you could go to jail for, but people do it all the time. Imagine eating bologna sandwiches and going potty out in the wide open for years on end just because you were bad at math.

We all hate taxes, we all do, taxes are horrible, horrible things. I mean, have you ever been inside of an H&R Block office? It looks like the room where convicted inmates get to visit with their families in prison, decorated with those fold-up chairs that people scratch their names into, glaring lights, and empty walls. And I'm sure H&R Block knows this, they're not trying to fool anybody by hanging a cherub poster on the wall and passing out wine and cheese. No, H&R Block is really Practice Prison; it's like a near-death experience in which the dead person catches a glimpse of hell and then comes back to life as a nice person. That's what H&R Block is, it's a lesson, like "You think paying taxes is bad? Try watching your mother sob uncontrollably as she sits on a chair with 'Alan is my bitch' scraped into the seat. Now how much did you really give to this Burrito of Hope charity?" I wish there was a box you could check that says, "I will be paying with A) a check, B) a credit card, or C) a pound of flesh." At least I could afford that to the extent I could remit some penalty fees, too.

This year, I got prepared. I watched the *Today* show every day and listened when Matt Lauer told me I was eligible for several significant deductions. I wrote them down and saved enough receipts to fuel Lindbergh's ticker-tape parade. Taxes, I had learned, were serious stuff. I had also been practicing with my husband, who, in the role of Lee, and me as myself, would act out the tragedy we named "Filing Your Taxes: A Melodrama," just to be really ready when the day of reckoning came:

LAURIE (as myself): Here you go, Lee. (Handing Lee a stack of imaginary papers.)

LEE (my husband): (Looks through imaginary papers.) Oh, boy. This doesn't look good. You're in very big trouble, like "bologna sandwich and exposed potty" trouble.

LAURIE: How much do we owe?

LEE: (Shaking his head.) More than you'll ever make in a lifetime. You could sell every egg in your ovaries and still not have enough.

LAURIE: What should we do? What are our options?

LEE: (Opens an imaginary cabinet, displaying a Colt .45, a noose, and a saber.) I'll let you use the noose in the office, but anything else you can take outside. I'm not a janitor, you know. I'm a numbers man.

LAURIE: There must be another way! There must be!

LEE: (Quietly leans over and opens the palm of his hand, which displays a package of airline peanuts from his last vacation.) Are you allergic?

LAURIE: (Gasps.) God forgive me! (Bites on the knuckle of her forefinger, turns away, and closes her eyes. Lights fade.)

When I finally went to Lee's office and sat in the chair across from him, my courage in a neat little ball in my lap, he ran down the list of my potential deductions.

"Have to be a practicing witch for that one," he said as he sliced across the entry with his pen. "Have to have ridden a donkey to the bottom of the Grand Canyon within the last twelve months for this one. And must have eaten a hot dog at a ballpark and become violently ill for that one."

"Bingo!" I said gleefully.

"Did you choke on a portion of the hot dog and lose consciousness at any point?" he added, looking above his glasses.

"No, because of that stupid stranger who beat on my back until that hot dog shot out of me like a baby!" I said sorrowfully.

"Then you only qualify for a partial deduction," he answered.

"How much do I owe?" I asked, wincing.

"Are you sure you didn't cast any spells in all of last year?" he asked. "Because if you did, I can get you to break even."

I thought for a moment. "Voodoo?" I asked. "I made a little doll of the president of our neighborhood association and sewed his lips shut!"

"We've got a winner," he said as he winked.

"Double, double, toil and trouble." I winked back.

Home Sweat Home

A bubble of sweat rolled down from my forehead, past the arch of my eyebrow, over the bridge of my nose, and parachuted into the inner corner of my left eye.

"It is *so hot*," I moaned as I lay motionless on my couch, then wiped the remaining drops of perspiration from my forehead.

"You've said that seventy-two times already today," my husband said slowly as he sat still in a chair. "I know it's hot. I'm three feet away from you."

"Why is it so hot?" I whined as I felt my insides slowly cooking.

"Because it's July and we live in the desert," he replied, turning to look at me with as little effort as possible. "And we don't have air-conditioning. Why is the front of your shirt all wet?"

"I have ice in my bra," I replied, closing my eyes as I felt another droplet speeding toward the right one.

"Do you think you have one that would fit me?" he asked.

My husband and I will be the first ones to admit that it was our fault. Who, in their right mind, buys a house in Phoenix without the necessity of air-conditioning?

We did. Chalk it up to ignorance, stupidity, or even love. We adored the little seventy-year-old bungalow so deeply that we bought it, despite the slow, unpredictable creak of the aging, corroded swamp cooler that rested on the roof.

Honestly, we weren't so idiotic that we actually thought we could live without air-conditioning; we had saved enough money to provide for a unit as well as some repairs that the house needed. But quickly, oh so quickly, the money slipped away as the plumbing needed replacing, the wiring needed updating, and a burglary forced us to install a security system and enough wrought iron around every door and window to build our own Eiffel Tower.

In April, I had kissed the last of the money good-bye in my accountant's office when he gently told me that my dog and cat could not be counted as dependents, and therefore the government was very, very angry with me.

"What's the matter?" I said to him as I wrote out the check. "Haven't you ever seen anyone cry before?"

"Yes," he replied quietly. "But no one's ever gotten sick in my wastebasket."

As the temperature outside started to rise, my husband and I got anxious. Our fears were confirmed when, on a 95-degree day, we turned on the decrepit swamp cooler and waited.

It hummed a little, spat, and fought with itself, and finally, a small little jet of air leaked from the vents enough to rustle some threads of dust that looked strangely like petrified farts hanging from the ceiling. We spent our food money for the next month on the services of a repairman who billed us $400 for a lot of imaginary work, but who did manage to get the cooler to shoot out enough hot air to cover us in the dust threads and what looked like asbestos.

"This is great," my husband, who is normally a very nice person, snapped. "Maybe the heat inside this house will work like radiation and kill the cancer we just got."

In what I thought was a valiant effort, my husband started working a tremendous amount of overtime so that we could buy an air conditioner.

"You are so wonderful," I said, giving him a kiss on the cheek. "With all of that overtime, how soon do you think we can get a new cooler?"

"I don't get overtime pay," he said, looking at me quizzically. "I just stay late and read magazines because it's seventy-two degrees in the office."

On a good day, the temperature inside our home was an even 100. With no sanctuary, I took to the couch, and wondered aloud how the people who built this house managed to stay alive during the summer. We already slept with wet sheets, wet hair, and wet clothes.

"Maybe we should have a séance and invite them back," my husband said from his chair. "If there were a couple of ghosts roaming around, at least we'd have some cold spots."

"Good idea, Sarah Winchester," I said. "I'll wait here while you get the Ouija board. In the meantime, you're hogging the fan."

"I am not. It's blowing more on you than it is on me. It's barely touching me!" my husband shot back.

"Liar!" I yelled. "There!! I just saw your hair move! It's totally blowing all over you! Selfish!"

"My hair!" he said, then pointed at me. "You hair is totally moving! It looks like you're in a hurricane over there!"

"You know what I think?" I asked. "I think you've had a heat stroke and are passive-aggressive! I never would have married you had I known you were a Fan Hogger!"

So there you have it. Our lives had literally boiled down to an argument over which one of us was sweating less. As a result, my husband received a blessing from the Pope, a nomination for a Nobel Peace Prize in the marital harmony division, and a gift certificate from World of Fans for not killing me with a handheld Vornado.

I, on the other hand, was very careful about how many dependents I claimed on my tax forms the next year, and with our refund money, we had a new cooler installed two weeks ago.

"Did you want to keep the old one and try to sell it?" the air-conditioning man asked me as he was about to pitch it from the roof.

"I couldn't do that to another human being," I said. "That thing is worth about as much as Mary Kay Letourneau's word."

"Actually, it would have worked a little better if there hadn't been that hole in your vent system," he informed me. " 'Bout as big as a man's head. You sure?"

I nodded as he began to push the old swamp cooler off.

"I've been to hell once," I said as it crashed to the ground and splintered into a hundred broken pieces. "It's just too damn hot to go there again."

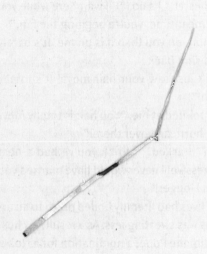

Spooky Little Girl Like You

I AM TELLING YOU FOR THE LAST TIME," my mother yelled from the living room, "there are NO SUCH things as ghosts. Now go back to bed before I take all of your friends home!"

I shuffled back to my bedroom, where my friends were waiting, and knew it was my own fault. We should have known better than to have a séance on Halloween, even if it was my birthday and I was having a slumber party.

Lots of people think it would be cool to have a birthday on Halloween, but it really isn't. Who would want to come to my house to play "Pin the Grin on the Pumpkin" when there were blocks of houses giving away free candy? Who was going to come to my house for a lousy piece of cake from Safeway when Milky Ways and Hershey bars were literally floating down the street?

As a result, only two of my fifth-grade classmates showed up at my house in costume on that Saturday night, out of the seven I had invited. My mom bought us pizza, then got all of us—my friends and my two younger sisters—ready for the annual trek down the street for the trick-or-treating bonanza. Since there were five of us, I had secretly hoped that we could all don white polyester gowns and go as Sister Sledge, belting out the chorus to "WE ARE FAMI-LEEE!" whenever anyone opened his door, but my mother shot me a look and put her hands on her hips.

"No, we are not doing that," she said sternly. "If you think I have time to stand here and braid all of your heads into cornfields, you've got another think coming!"

My friend Jamie came to my party as a witch anyway, and my other friend, Kassie, came in a rhinestone-cowboy outfit, mainly because her father owned horses and she rode in competitions. Since I had bet all of my options on the Sister Sledge theme, I had to come up with something quick, or my mom would throw a Hefty bag over my head and make me go as trash.

"What am I going to be?" I whined, going through my closet.

My mother grabbed a pencil and a spiral notebook and handed it to me. "Just be Anne Frank again," she said as I sulked.

"I was Anne Frank last year!" I whined.

"It's Anne Frank or the trash bag," my mother offered. "That little girl stayed in the attic for a *long time*; you can be her for two years in a row!"

My mom stood close by us as we went trick-or-treating from house to house, smoking a cigarette near the curb as we knocked on each door.

"Let me see your candy," she demanded after every treat. "That woman's a nutjob. Did she try to give you an apple? Did her house smell funny?"

When we returned to our own house, my mother cut the cake and I opened presents. I got a can of Love's Baby Soft, a bottle of Charlie, and a forty-five of "Play That Funky Music, White Boy," which we took into my room immediately because we heard there was a dirty word sung on it.

Jamie, Kassie, and I were listening to the record over and over again, but since we had no idea what the word might be, we got bored pretty quickly.

"Let's have a séance!" I said suddenly, and Jamie turned off the lights.

"What do we say?" Kassie said, her rhinestone hat still shining in the dark.

"How about, 'Oh spirits, come down and have some of Laurie's birthday cake,'" Jamie replied.

"That's good," I agreed. "Have some of my birthday cake and tell us what the dirty word in the song is. . . ." I trailed off, trying to be spooky.

"Come to the slumber party, spirits," Kassie said, laughing. "We'll give you candy!"

We were all giggling when suddenly, the closed door to my bedroom swung open, hitting the wall behind it, slammed shut, swung open, shut, open . . . shut.

We were quiet for a moment, and then we screamed. We had all seen it, we had all seen the same thing. The door swinging open by itself, shutting by itself, and each time it swung open again, we could see the brightly lit hallway and the fact that it was empty. There was no one there.

It was Jamie who ran to the light switch and turned it on. "Oh my God" was all she said.

"Mom!" I yelled, getting up and running into the living room, where my parents were. "Mom! My door opened!"

"Go back to bed," she instructed. "We're watching Sonny and Cher!"

"It opened by itself," I insisted. "It opened and slammed shut by itself!"

"I told you she was getting weirder," my mother said to my father, then pointed to me. "If you keep acting this way, no one will want to marry you when you grow up! No one marries a nutjob! And you're not living here for the rest of your life!"

"We all saw it, Mrs. Notaro," Jamie said from the hallway.

My mother looked at my father. "All right," she complied. "Go get your trick-or-treat bags, and empty them on the floor."

We did what she said, and my mom started looking at every piece of candy, even the cheap saltwater taffy pieces, which we never would have eaten.

"What are you doing?" my father asked her.

"Remember Art Linkletter's daughter?" she whispered, even though we could hear her. "Look for anything with the letters L, S, and D on it. That nutjob down the street probably slipped them a chocolate mickey! You girls stay off of the roof, you hear me?"

She didn't find anything, and I knew she wouldn't. When I insisted one last time that there really was a ghost in my room, she threatened to take my friends home.

"She has a very vivid imagination," I heard her say to my father as I shuffled back to my bedroom. "Remember when we went camping last year and that cow bumped into the trailer and she started screaming that it was Bigfoot? Yes, you do so remember!"

When I got back to my bedroom, Jamie and Kassie had already started pulling my desk across the carpet. We closed the door again, very gently, pushed the desk against it, and then tried very, very hard to go to sleep.

The Little King

The very second that the automatic door swung open at the mega-super-plus toy store, my eardrums exploded from the high-pitched screaming that came from within it. I was scared. I braced myself, took a deep breath, and then a step.

Inside, the air was thick and muggy with the perspiration of hyperactive children. They ran from one aisle to the other discharging sound barrier–breaking squeals as they climbed over little gyms, rode bicycles, and toppled displays with the same ferocity the Nazis used when they destroyed France. Parents, clearly the innocent civilians in the scenario, hid in dark corners, plastic playhouses, tents, and on the book aisle. They huddled closely together, their eyes wide, collectively pushing terrified newcomer parents out of their sanctuaries with the words, "There's no more room! We'll be discovered! We heard there's an empty box on aisle nine with an open spot!"

I had to go into the store; I had no choice. I had upset the Little King on Thanksgiving, and I only had one way to get back into his Royal Highness's good graces.

A Little King's ransom in Christmas presents.

You have to appease the Little King.

As soon as he struts through the door, the atmosphere changes.

Every member of my family becomes a servant, footman, lady-in-waiting, all eager to serve our thirty-three-pound master.

"Would an audience with Elmo please Your Highness?"

"You require someone to fetch your chocolate milk, sir? Pick me! Pick me!"

"Absolutely, we must destroy the talking Barney doll that Grandpa paid a hundred and twenty dollars for by kicking it repeatedly. It frightens me, too, sire. Shall we employ this metal lamp base to crush its skull?"

He'll tell us where to sit, mutely pointing at a couch, a chair, or, if you've angered the Little King, the floor. You can be banished for simply sitting in the wrong place, talking to him without being addressed first, or merely suggesting that it isn't particularly a good idea to rub purple Play-Doh into my mother's beige carpeting.

We all try to please the Little King, known to the outside world as my two-year-old nephew, Nicholas. He makes his demands in the language of the Little King, a dialect we have been forced to become as fluent in as we are our native tongue.

"Num-num gigee peepah me!" is easily understood to us as "It is none other than a necessity to have the presence of my giraffe and my pacifier while I dine on pizza. And I mean NOW."

"Woo-woo rah eebah tub help!" means simply, "I must have my dog, lion, and zebra in my bath, and I demand you to assist me in gathering them. And I mean NOW."

The Little King gets his way, and will not hesitate to vomit if he doesn't, emitting two distinct warning gags before the retch is complete. He also won't hesitate to humiliate you if his demands are not met. A few weeks ago at Thanksgiving, I went to the bathroom after dinner, and while I was conducting business (number one), the door suddenly swung open and there he stood.

I immediately pointed to the door and said, "See-see toonoo Orie bubbo nah! [You are not supposed to see Aunt Laurie on the potty!]"

"Num-num rah Orie Nick pay peese ow [Jester Laurie, you must return to court at this moment and engage me in the game of lion and giraffe, when I will continually chase you until that herniated disk in your lower back pops out and shatters a window like a baseball]," the Little King said.

"Pe fo fo [Not now]," I said, attempting to cover my hindquarters. "Orie um . . . tee-tee [I'm, um . . . tinkling]."

He looked at me slightly out of the corner of his eye, opened the door, and left.

"What is Aunt Laurie doing in there?" my mother asked when he returned to the dining room.

He scrunched up his face so hard it turned red and said simply "GRRR!" in a hearty grunt.

"You did a doody in front of the baby?" my mother screamed when I returned to the table. "What kind of weirdo, sicko thing is that? Is that how you get your kicks?! ANIMAL!"

Because my family tended to believe a toddler's word over my own, as punishment I was called to the head of the table by the Little King, where I was commanded to perform a sullen little jig in front of my entire family as he shouted, "Da! Da! [Dance, you silly half-wit, dance!]"

Apparently, it wasn't enough. If I dare speak to him or say his name aloud, he will look at me sternly, shout "No, bad Orie!" and point to the floor, where my proper place is.

Sitting between a haggled mother of four with a stress-related skin condition and a weeping single dad inside the empty box on aisle nine, I wondered which was worse: being torn limb from limb by ravenous children who had mistaken me for a life-size Teletubby or trying to shovel mashed potatoes between a little metal slit after I've been pronounced "the Aunt in the Iron Mask."

With only one of my feet outside the box, an angry mob of children charged, misidentified me as a parent, and began screaming, "Buy this for me!" I dashed down the aisle, and in a mad haste grabbed the first box I could get my arms around and rushed toward the checkout.

It was only when I reached my car that I realized how lucky I was. Looking at the package, I saw the words "Ball Pit Jungle Gym Carnival," and realized that this, indeed, was the only toy in the entire universe that the Little King did not already count among his possessions.

As I lifted the massive box out of the cart and into the backseat of my car, the herniated disk popped out of my back, but I continued to struggle until I was able to close the car door.

I got in the driver's seat and wiped my brow. I had done it. The Little King would be pleased, and I, in return, wouldn't have to eat Christmas dinner in the garage next to a space heater.

Suddenly, the box shifted in the backseat, and seemingly began to move on its own.

"Hey! Are we safe? Did we get out?" I heard a parent say. "Can we go back and get my husband? He's lying at the bottom of an inflatable canoe on aisle three."

What's on That Dog's Butt?

The wood floor of my living room was littered with little, fluffy white things.

I saw it when I woke up and was shuffling to the kitchen to make my morning tea.

I saw a bit of the fluffy mass float through the air and land on the head of my "dog," Bella, whom my husband and I have come to believe is not a canine at all, but a secret government experiment gone horribly wrong.

Bella looked at me and panted as a larger piece of white fuzz dangled from her lip.

Then I saw it. The sight was chilling. There, near the foot of the couch, lay the carcass of Bella's "Baby," once a cute little fleece alligator. I bought Baby for Bella when she was a wee little puppy and still exhibited signs of being a normal dog, hours before she had developed the potential to terrorize what she laughingly calls "her masters." The shell of Baby was now hollow, gutted like a deer, her hide crumpled and limp, lying tragically on the floor.

"Squeak! Squeak! Squeak!" Bella said to me as her fatal fangs repeatedly bit into the round, plastic bubble that had once been Baby's squeaky heart.

I screamed in horror and called for my husband. "The dingo ate her Baby!" I yelled. "The dingo ate her Baby!"

My husband jumped out of bed and ran into the living room. "That's it!" he said when he saw the puffy mess. "Last week she ate my favorite shoe and yesterday she ate two whole packs of Juicy Fruit that I left on the coffee table! It got stuck to the bottom of my shoes and when I was at school that morning, I realized I had dragged a six-foot banner from the Association of Blind Students halfway across campus! Even the Hare Krishnas stopped singing to laugh at me!"

Bella didn't care that my husband, an innocent college student, was now considered the mysterious, dark-force enemy of the blind.

"Squeak! Squeak! Squeak!" she said.

I was bound and determined to punish her for her bad deed, and I put her outside for the rest of the day.

"That's it for you!" I said as I shook my finger at her. "Your Baby is dead!! I'm not buying you any more victims!"

As soon as she came in that afternoon, she catapulted herself onto our other, older and nearly mummified dog, Chigger. Once a cheerful, vibrant, happy Labrador, Chigger doubled her body weight once we got Bella and she started eating her way through subsequent depression. She spends the majority of her day hiding beneath the coffee table or under the cushions of the couch, much like prey does, trying to blend in and afraid to make a single move to indicate any sign of life to her predator, Bella.

To make matters worse, I suspected that Chigger wasn't long for this world, as I had spotted a growth of sorts on her rear end several days before. I thought perhaps she had taken a particularly strained movement, but every time I tried to check it out, she either sat down or her fat shifted over the part I needed to see. I could tell that the tumor was gray and rather oval-shaped, a little bit smaller than an egg, but I needed help lifting her up so I could get a better look.

As Bella tugged on Chigger's foot, the poor, chunky, graying dog threw once last glance at me for rescue, and then went limp.

Before I could even reach her, Bella pounced on Chig's jelly belly with a forceful hop.

My husband gasped. "She's trying to make Chigger squeak!" he said.

Suddenly, I remembered the butt tumor and told my husband, but as we tried to get to it, Chigger remained as stationary as the Sphinx, and my husband suggested that the only way to reach her behind was to rent a crane or prop her up with lumber.

Bella went for Chigger's tummy again.

"EEEEEK!" Chig yelped as the air rushed out of her.

"Don't we have a live wire or a knife that Bella can play with?" my husband cried.

"She ate our knives," I said as I picked up my car keys. "I'll be right back."

As I stood in front of the fleece doggie toys fifteen minutes later at the pet store, I spotted an alligator and I grabbed it. I tested its life force; it squeaked gleefully. I was paying for the new Baby when I spotted the pink ball, and thought perhaps that was what I needed to run Bella's batteries down.

The minute I pulled it out of the bag, she knew it was for her. Miraculously, the pink ball caught Chigger's eye, too, and all three of us headed for the backyard to play catch.

Chigger never had a chance. It was a pitiable sight as she tried to run, resembling a rolling fur and fat wave. Although the look on her face joyfully exclaimed, "I'm RUNNING! I'm RUNNING! I am ALIVE!" she lumberingly covered only about six inches of ground before Bella caught the ball. I had to turn my head to laugh at my poor, old, near-dead dog.

With her false sense of ability and failing eyesight, Chigger convinced herself that a rotting, brown orange that had fallen from our citrus tree last season was indeed the pink ball, and dropped the fetid fruit at my feet to throw again. Give a dying dog with a tumor on her butt a last wish, I said to myself.

Then I had an idea.

As I pretended to throw the orange again, I waited until Chigger hauled her body mass a foot or so, and then I snuck up behind her. While she was carefully sniffing around for the orange, I grabbed her tail with one hand and her butt with the other before she had a chance to sit.

And then I found that tumor.

It was flat, fleshy, and when I pinched it, a part of it came off in my hands, and I thought, Well, what do you know? This part of her is dead already! and I moved in for a better view.

The tumor was puckered where I had pinched it, and it sure was sticky. And pliable.

And rather pleasant-smelling.

I had no choice but to pull the mass of the equivalent of six chewed-up pieces of Juicy Fruit in one, tough yank before Chigger took the opportunity to sit down again.

"EEEEEK!" she yelped.

Red Mice

After I woke up on Saturday morning and was making my usual shuffle to the bathroom, I heard a voice from the living room call, "Don't go in there. We have a problem."

It was my husband, sitting in a chair, facing a blank and silent TV screen.

He looked mad.

"What kind of problem?" I asked.

"The kind of problem that forces you to go out into the backyard and dig a hole," he answered plainly.

My heart dropped to my stomach. This wasn't good, and as my face flushed in panic, I opened the bathroom door. There was water everywhere.

I took a deep breath. This was bad. In our house, we only have one bathroom, which means if it's out of order, we're out of luck.

"I used Drano already," my husband said as he came over to stand behind me. "It's just not going down. The toilet won't flush, and the plunger won't work."

"What should we do?" I asked.

My husband sighed. "Either we call a plumber," he answered, "or we have an alternative option."

"Such as?" I asked.

He led me to the window that faced the backyard and opened the curtains. Next to Turd Alley, the strip of dirt that my dogs defecate in, is what we tenderly call "The Structure." Apparently, it had once been a garage that was in use for decades until large pieces of it began falling off and termites munched on what was left. As a result, I believe the only thing keeping it erect is prayer, mostly on the part of my neighbor, whose fence will be flattened a moment after The Structure takes its last breath. The garage door is slightly open and also frozen in place with rust and decay, so access inside is rather difficult, unless you're an advanced yogi who can twist his body like a pretzel and also possess absolutely no fear of black widow spiders and scorpions. It was directly in front of this slightly ajar door that I saw a large mound of dirt that looked like a grave.

"What's that?" I asked, pointing to it.

"I dug a very deep hole," my husband answered, somewhat beaming with pride. "It will take us months to fill it up!"

I thought for a moment. "You made us an . . . outhouse?" I questioned, hoping that I had misunderstood. "In The Structure?"

"If it works in the mountains, it can work in the city," he asserted.

"I'm calling a plumber," I said, reaching for the phone book. "I'll be damned if my white heinie ever sees the light of day! The Structure barely has a roof on it!"

So I called the plumber, who told me he could be out in about two hours. In the meantime, my husband jumped ship under the guise of going to work and left me to fend for myself.

I tried to wait for the plumber, but I couldn't. I hadn't tinkled since the night before, and my bladder felt as heavy and big as a watermelon. At the last minute, I ran out to The Structure to relieve myself, but despite sucking in my breath and getting my knee all the way to my ear, my time was running out and my bladder was running out of patience. I tried in vain to force the door open further, but it was no use. The flood was coming, and there was nowhere to hide. With only seconds to spare, I hopped into Turd Alley, leaned against an orange tree, unbuttoned, and squatted. My dogs, however, thought this was a game. While the bigger one kept jumping on me, the puppy equated my release with the new trick she had learned, drinking out of the hose, and tried repeatedly to get her fill. As I grabbed hold of her to push her out of the spray, I peed on my own hand, on my shoe, and then stepped into a pile of fresh doody that wasn't mine. I had already wiped and rebuttoned when I noticed my neighbor, curiously looking out her second-story window down into my yard.

The plumber finally showed up, and I showed him the problem. He seemed to know how to fix it right away, and climbed on the roof to insert a chain into the sewer line.

Then the phone rang, and it was my friend Jamie. I told her about my potty problems, and that Mrs. Parrish had seen me urinating on my dog.

"You know what that sounds like to me," Jamie said, "that sounds like feminine problems. My plumber had to do the same thing with the chain, and when he pulled it out, there were hundreds of tampons hanging off that thing like ornaments on a Christmas tree."

I gasped. I had come face-to-face with this plumber; he would know they were mine. This was something I couldn't blame on my husband.

I hung up the phone and ran outside to where the plumber was perched on the roof.

"Guess what?" I yelled as loud as I could, trying to scream over the sound of the drilling chain. "My husband has a very big problem! He sleepwalks, and once I caught him flushing a whole box of tampons down the toilet! I said, 'What are you, crazy! You're not supposed to flush tampons! I never do!' Isn't that funny!"

He just looked at me, and I went back into the house.

When the drilling stopped, the plumber came inside and wrote out a report.

"Your sewer line was clogged," he said. "Probably has a lot to do with tree roots. You've got a pine tree right over that pipe."

"Oh thank God," I said, breathing a sigh of relief. "Only tree roots."

"Yeah," he said, filling out the form. "Sign right here, please. See, the biggest problem with that is that the roots catch all kinds of stuff, and then you get a clog, and then your toilet backs up."

"Did you find a clog?" I said slowly.

"Found a clump," he replied. "Big as my head. What you could call a whole colony of red mice."

"Mice?" I asked. "In the sewer?"

"Red mice," the plumber said with a grin. "You know. Tampons."

I just stood there, not able to say anything.

"You really shouldn't flush them," the plumber said, handing me the receipt. "Make sure you tell your husband that."

And then he winked.

The Hands of Death

I didn't understand it. The pumpkin heads were *right there*.

They were *right there*, right where I had put them on the top shelf in the laundry room last year.

Now, they were gone.

And I had a feeling I knew who was responsible.

"Honey!" I yelled to my husband, who was very busy trying to figure out the instructions for the new stereo he had just bought. "Have you seen my pumpkin heads?"

If anything in my house is missing, mutilated, or downright killed below knee level, I know the culprit is Bella, our dwarf Wookie with a severe case of separation anxiety, who appeared to be a dog at the pound, from whence she was then passed on to us.

However, if anything is missing from above knee level, there's only one person who knows about it, and is hiding the details because he's too afraid to tell his wife.

I feared that the pumpkin heads had met the fate of the Man Hands, the same instruments of destruction that turn an entire load of white clothes the same Strawberry Quik shade of pink; the same ten fingers that believe in each of their ten hearts that they can successfully make ice, yet flagrantly return the ice trays to the freezer with a quarter of an inch of water in each of the wells; the same appendages that, last January, headed out into the front yard clutching a hedge clipper to assist them in cutting the Christmas lights down; and, oh yes, the very same agents of Satan that knocked off an antique light sconce with a hand-blown glass shade, which then shattered upon impact with the floor in a record twenty-four seconds after I put it up. "Now that cannot be my fault," the Man Hands said, looking at the glass shards on the floor. "I had no idea it was there and was just walking down the hallway."

"Why were you touching the walls, then?" I callously asked. "Why do the Man Hands feel the need to touch the walls? Keep the Man Hands in your pockets. They are not butterflies, they are not balloons, they are not cute little birds that flutter about. Those hands are the Apocalypse!"

My husband does not have the Midas touch. Unfortunately, he was blessed with the gentle caress of Godzilla, which really only surfaces when he comes into contact with anything that's mine. In any case, I feared that the pumpkin heads had met their fate at the same moment the Man Hands came to lie upon them; although I hoped I was wrong, I knew in my suspicious heart that it was true.

I needed the pumpkin heads, and had intended to use them as my centerpiece ever since I kind of committed to decorating the house after a neighbor commented on the sad, dead state of our lawn several weeks ago.

"If it wasn't for the severed sections of Christmas lights still hanging there, people would think your house was vacant," my neighbor said as he unrolled a length of silver tape to prevent birds from flocking on his winter lawn. I had to admit that it was kind of true, since I had completely given up on our yard after I got a water bill for $150 in July and had never seen our grass take on anything beyond a sickly lime hue.

"Oh, we're getting ready for Halloween," I quickly said. "We decided last Halloween to hand out candy as Herman and Lily Munster this year, and wanted the experience to be very authentic. Look at the cobwebs on my porch! It's taken every bit of will I had not to brush them away this whole, entire year! And the dead rosebushes, a tragedy, but a sacrifice I was willing to make. It's all for the kids, you know."

"You don't have kids," he replied.

"We know people who do," I stammered.

So in the effort to make good on my lie, I hit the stores in search of the perfect decorations to turn our neglected, trashy home into a haunted one. I bought orange lights to replace the cut-up Christmas ones, a big fake spider to go with my already cultured-cobweb porch, and a five-foot-tall skeleton with eyes that light up.

I rushed home with my purchases, anxious to set up my display on the front porch, and that's when I discovered the missing pumpkin heads.

"Where are the pumpkin heads?" I asked my husband as he shuffled into the laundry room. "I put them right up here!"

His head hung low, and he shrugged. "I'll buy you new ones," he offered.

"Like the Christmas lights?" I said. "So, you've killed again. What happened this time?"

"They *attacked* me," he said, flailing around the Man Hands for effect.

"The pumpkin heads attacked you," I repeated, trying to stay calm.

"YES!" he answered, and began to reenact the scenario right before my very eyes.

"I was outside," he continued as he opened the laundry room door and stood on the other side of it. "And it was really hot, it was July, and I had just taken the trash out. I was coming back inside and—"

He swung the door into the laundry room, and suddenly the door stopped, as if it was blocked by something big and invisible. "And suddenly, the door wouldn't open any farther, and I realized that there was something trapped in between the door and the dryer."

I just stood, looking at him.

"It was the pumpkin heads," he explained, as if I didn't get it. "They must have fallen off of the shelf and just got lodged there."

I kept looking at him.

"It was hot outside," he said again. "It was really hot."

"So you bludgeoned the pumpkin heads with the door to get back inside?" I asked.

"YES!" he affirmed. "The smiling head was cracked in three pieces, so I threw them away."

"*Them?*" I asked.

"They were attached," he said. "Weren't they?"

"Idiot," I said as I walked out of the laundry room, through the dining room, and almost to the bedroom before I heard the sound of a crash, the signal that Man Hands had killed yet again.

The Slattern's Blue Panties

It was lying at the bottom of the dryer, curled up, all nice and snugly, like it belonged there.

Like it shouldn't have been any place else.

I saw it after I collected my clothes from the dryer that required the dry cleaning I'm too cheap to pay for. I figured out that if you throw the clothes in with a wet dishcloth and a Downy sheet (luckily plucked from a box that my friend Kate left at my house when her washing machine broke), they get steamed, almost like a pot sticker, and reemerge with considerably less odor, wrinkles, and pet hair.

But the parcel I had found, however, wasn't any of the items from which I had just eliminated what my husband calls "the homeless aroma."

I didn't recognize it, and I realized this as I pulled it from the dryer bottom and examined it in my hands.

They were blue and shiny.

And they were panties. Ladies' panties. With a waistband that was still intact, definite proof that they had never been on my body.

Initially, I was very confused. I didn't understand. Then, like a bolt of lightning from Sally Jesse Raphael, it hit me.

MY HUSBAND WAS HAVING AN AFFAIR. I knew it. I *knew* it. Only last week, I saw a show on Sally with a panel of "experts" (women who had been cheated on or had done the cheating) and they all said the same thing: "Don't ignore the signs. The truth will set you free to claim half his earnings!"

Being the shallow sort of person that I am, I scrambled to find the tag.

Damn! I said to myself when I found it and read "Victoria's Secret." Damn! The hussy had better underwear than me! I wear Fruit of the Loom, which I had apparently confused with "sexy" since they completely cover and hide from view the double-decker jelly-belly rolls that comprise my torso.

Victoria's Secret? I thought again. That's not his type! A girl that shaves and possibly waxes and plucks? AND does laundry at MY house? AND DOES LAUNDRY!!!!

I tried to tell myself to calm down, that there had to be some rational explanation. My husband would never do such a thing. Never, I said inside my head, I light up his life! I give him hope to carry on! That man lives like a KING! And besides, he's afraid of me!

Then a thought popped in my head. Bing! It has to be my best friend Jamie's underwear, and I must have picked up her clothes by mistake when we were on vacation in San Francisco. I breathed a sigh of relief and kind of laughed to myself. He's not having an affair. He's too lazy! He's a bum! The King can't even wash a dish; he's never located enough energy to finish painting the outside of the house, let alone go through the trouble of sneaking around with a high-maintenance girl who plucks and shaves! *Too much trouble.* If it ever happened, I'd have to be the one to set it all up, introduce them to one another, arrange all the dates, go to Victoria's Secret and buy her *more* fancy underwear, keep nagging him incessantly, "Get off that rump roast, go to the pay phone, and CALL YOUR GIRLFRIEND!!!" and then I'd end up driving him there and plugging in the fifty cents myself. "Hi, Slovenly Woman? My husband is *yearning* for you!"

He'd never have an affair!

But I had to confirm it, just for peace of mind, and to see if the truth would set me free from my obligatory twelve nights a year, if only as an act of revenge.

"Hi!" I said into the phone. "Do you have a blue pair of Victoria's Secret underwear?"

"Good God, no!" my best friend Jamie shot back over the phone from Los Angeles. "You have to shave with those things, otherwise stuff just pokes out *everywhere!*"

"Oh," I said simply.

"Why?" she asked. "Did you find some?"

I guess she could hear me nodding.

There was a pause. "That's not good," Jamie finally said. "Do you think he's . . ."

I guess she heard me nodding again.

"Oh, that's insane!" she told me. "You light up his life! You give him hope to carry on! He lives like a king! Besides, he's completely afraid of you. I once heard him say that he'd rather eat his own eyes than beat you to the bathroom in the morning! He said he'll just lay in bed and hold it until either you wake up or he cries from the pain!"

"Didn't you see Sally's show on Sneaky, Sex-Crazed Spouses? The experts said not to ignore the signs!" I pouted. "Strange underwear in my house is a red flag, don't you think?"

"Did you *see* those 'expert' women? Who wouldn't cheat on them?" asserted my best friend. "They had teeth like Jewel! They could cut lumber with those fangs!"

"Wait, wait, wait," I said slowly. "This might not be all that bad. If I confronted him with the evidence, maybe I could play the guilt card. Just think of all the possibilities!"

"Wow," Jamie marveled. "That's genius! Those panties are like a transferable gift certificate to Crate and Barrel!"

"And for handyman and maid services! I'm going to make him take down the Christmas lights from last year and then make him put them right back up!" I exclaimed. "I gotta go! I'm going to get out the paintbrushes and ladder right now! By this time to-morrow, I can start telling people where I live again!"

"Send him over here when you're done," Jamie said excitedly.

"Oh," I chuckled. "He'll never be done!"

Before I had a chance to hang up, however, the call-waiting beeped and I said good-bye quickly and switched lines.

"Hi, are you free tonight?" a sultry, sexy, deep voice said. "I was wondering if I could come over to do some laundry."

It was the Victoria's Secret vixen, mistaking me for my husband. I knew it! Another sign!

"Sorry, slutty!" I yelled into the phone. "You can't have what's not yours!! He's MINE!!! Go find your own slave!"

"Dork," the sultry voice said, sounding a little puzzled. "It's Kate! I don't want your husband! I just want my box of Downy and my underwear back that I left there! It's my best pair!"

White Noise, White Soap, and Man Desire: Marriage Advice from Two Mean Girls

So, are you ready to get married?" I asked my best friend, Jeff, as he, my other best friend, Jamie, and I sat down to eat lunch at a sidewalk café in Pasadena. I had flown to California for somewhat of a last hurrah, since he was the final one of us to tie the knot and would be a married man by the month's end.

Jeff looked puzzled. "I'm *ready*," he snapped as he spread a napkin over his lap. "I bought an extra pillow."

Jamie and I looked at each other and burst out laughing. We could tell that our little friend had some very lofty ideas about sharing your life with someone as if you were the only one that mattered; just like a man.

"Kristin's the nice partner," Jeff explained about his betrothed. "I'm the bossy one. She understands that. We have that understanding."

"None of us is the nice partner in our relationships," Jamie added. "All three of us are the mean one. But that doesn't matter. Things still change."

"Like you might as well get rid of all of your CDs now, because in two weeks, she'll think that they all suck," I said.

"And you should carry roughly five dollars in quarters with you at all times so you can call her from wherever you are," Jamie added.

"And instead of falling asleep to music, it will be white noise," I quipped. "Women need that. I have a fan."

"I have a wave machine. Happy hour will be a thing of the past. There's something you do instead now," Jamie inserted. "It's called dinner at home."

"And after you come home from work or after five o'clock," I stated, "you need to ask her if you want to go back out again."

"Unless she sends you to the store," Jamie mentioned.

"Unless she sends you to the store," I confirmed.

"Forget about being the first one to get the mail anymore," Jamie said. "You'll never get unhandled mail again."

"And if you find jelly or ice cream on the remote control," I insisted, "it's a totally natural thing."

"After you get married, you'll never be as funny at home as you are at work," Jamie added.

"And when she laughed at your jokes before, she was faking it," I said.

"Once you've told a story, you need to retire it," Jamie announced. "Because every time she hears a story more than once, she'll hate you a little more and a little more."

"And never read to her from a book or magazine article aloud," I declared. "She'll never think it's as interesting as you do."

"If she gets sick," Jamie said, "you have to hold her hair and clean it up and then kiss her afterward."

"But other than that instance, if you're initiating the kiss, you need to brush your teeth first," I added.

"Her sexual obligation to you expires in two years," Jamie stated. "And should she decide to oblige you after that, you should be very, *very* grateful."

"And you're never allowed to say 'boink,' 'pork,' 'do it,' or 'get it on,'" I informed Jeff. "Or wake her up in the middle of the night when you're . . . overwhelmed by your . . . man desire."

"You could get suspended for that," Jamie whispered.

"If she's not talking to you, like when she's reading a book or watching TV, that means she's BUSY." I nodded. "And *you* need to be quiet."

"And when you feel the need to go to the bathroom, you should ask her if she needs to go first," Jamie announced.

"But you should really try to make it a point to do the 'big things' someplace else before you get home," I declared.

"But if you do it at home by accident," Jamie said carefully, "never, never call her in to look at it. It's gross and will entirely change her perspective of you."

"She'll see you as the animal that you are," I stated.

"The animal that you are," Jamie agreed.

"And if there's some potato chips or cookies in a bag, don't eat them," I said. "She might not be done with them, and may want them at some point. Just because there's food in the house doesn't mean it's fair game."

"And if she asks you if you want to share a dessert at a restaurant, that means she wants some," Jamie added. "And it's in your best interest to say yes."

"And when you're at your parents' house and she yawns for the first time, it means it's time to go," I said.

"If the phone rings and you don't think it's for you," Jamie added, "you still have to answer it anyway."

"If she ever comes home and there's a drunk guy on the couch and another one throwing up in the bathroom, expect to be in trouble," I informed him.

"If she buys a bar of soap that isn't white, it is not for you," Jamie stated.

"And if she asks you to do several things, it's not okay to just do the last thing she said because that's the only one you remember," I asserted.

"Be honest with yourself; set the alarm for the time the Real You will get up, not the Ambitious You, because the Ambitious You doesn't really exist," Jamie added.

"At night, if she takes the covers, just get used to being cold," I stated. "It's more important for her to be warm. A simple draft can render her infertile, and then your family name will die with you."

"And that's selfish," Jamie added.

"That's selfish," I agreed.

Jeff stared at us for a long, long time, trying to take it all in. As I studied his face, I got the impression as he furrowed his brow and crinkled his mouth that he was about to cry. Suddenly, I panicked. Had we said too much? Had we been too honest? Had we scared him horribly? Was he thinking about jumping ship? I looked at Jamie, and realized that she was looking at me with the same awful look on her face that I had on mine.

What had we done? We *were* the mean ones, after all!

"Maybe you're right," he finally said. "Maybe I'm not so ready. How could I be so stupid? What am I thinking! Am I OUT OF MY MIND?!"

Jamie and I didn't know what to say. We just sat there, horrified, our mouths hanging open, getting ready to protest. WHAT HAD WE DONE?

"I don't have any extra pillowcases!" Jeff proclaimed as he stomped his foot, and then looked at us, smiling wickedly.

As Time Goes By

It is 10 P.M. WHERE IS HE?

I light another cigarette and tap my foot against the floor. He is already half an hour late coming home from work. My husband had called earlier that afternoon, saying that he would be home at nine-thirty. Sometimes he stops at the store for beer, I remind myself, maybe that's what he did. But my foot keeps tapping.

I recognize my behavior as the Sort-of, Kind-of Worried Phase, and I try to calm myself down. As the hands of the clock inch their way into the future, I know I have to stay rational. What's half an hour? I tell myself. The line at the store could have been very long, it's Saturday night. He may have been caught in a drunk-driving checkpoint on his way home from Tempe. Maybe he was hungry and decided to stop and get a hamburger, right?

There's a million reasons for him to be a half hour late.

You are your mother's daughter, I remind myself, don't buy into it. When I lived at home and was even ten minutes late, my mother was already making arrangements at the funeral home and would pull out the pink taffeta dress I refused to wear at the prom, determined to finally get her money's worth by burying me in it. "Late equals dead," she would pound into my head over the years, saying it every time she emerged from the darkness like a phantom when I tried to sneak in the house at night.

All of her fear paid off like the lottery one evening when a uniformed officer knocked on the front door and, when she answered it, showed her my driver's license. She was already on her way to the floor with her eyes rolled back in her head by the time the officer explained he had simply found my wallet in a parking lot, where I had carelessly dropped it.

The cycle stops here, my brain commands me, but when I hear the chime of the clock screaming at me that it is ten-fifteen, I throw myself immediately into the Anger Phase.

What the hell is he doing going to the store without calling me first! Now he's forty-five minutes late! The selfish bastard! His need for beer supersedes my worry? Boy, he's really going to get it this time. Sleeping on the couch with the dog's blanket. I'll blow my nose on his pillow! I'm going to hide his cigarettes, put a chair in front of the door, and turn off all the lights so he hurts his knee when he walks in! HA! That will teach him to be late!

I stop, and then gasp with a long, deep breath. I know what he's doing!

He's having an affair! With this single thought, I make the natural, unnoticeable transition to the Accusatory Stage, where my mind gathers up all of my rational thoughts in a ball and shoves them underneath the couch, right next to where my dog keeps her reserve stash of dried-up cat shits.

He thinks he can get away with this, huh? That's why he took a shower and wore clean underwear to work! That's why he asked me if he was getting old-man hairs in his ears! I run outside and stand by the side of the road, looking down the street for headlights that look like his truck's.

Don't be ridiculous! my logic tells me. It's ten-twenty. He can't be having an affair! He's getting old-man hairs in his ears! Besides, he's lying on the side of the freeway after a horrific car accident, his last words leaking out of his mouth, "Tell Laurie . . . I love her . . . and that I never thought she was fat . . . I like big butts . . ."

I leap off the edge of the Accusatory Stage and find myself

completely submerged in the Full-on Freak-out Phase, completely bypassing the obligatory Prepanic Phase.

My husband is dead. I am a widow. I am alone. The police will be coming soon; who do I call? Do I start calling hospitals, do I call his mother? Should I change into something black now, I just got a new black dress! I'll have to start dating again! I'm going to have to go on a diet! Oh my God. I no longer have a scapegoat!

I know he's dead. He's almost an hour late, of course he's dead. I see myself kneeling by his casket, holding his hand for the last time, wondering why he's wearing my pink taffeta prom gown.

My stomach sinks, my hands go white with cold blood, fear crawls into my throat. I keep looking down the street, headlights approach, I'm shaking, the car passes, it's a minivan. What do I do?

I think, calm yourself down; if he's dead, you can buy a really nice car with the insurance money. You can have the sofa re-covered. In *velvet*. Think of how much money you'll save on food, he eats (ate) like a prisoner! You can stretch out in bed! That will fill the empty spot in your life caused by his death!

More headlights approach. I wait anxiously, almost jumping up and down. It's a Dodge Dart with no hubcaps.

Then I start bargaining. Please let him be okay, I start to mutter, please let him be okay. I'll do anything. I'll stop picking my face, even if I really do think I have a 40 to 60 percent chance of getting something good out and have access to a mirror with lighting that is simply unparalleled; I'll start letting people in during heavy traffic, well, all except city buses, because you could get stuck behind one for a good five to seven minutes, maybe even nine if there's a bike rider on board who has to get off and then unlatch his bike from the front of the bus, and that's flatly too long to ask for any do-gooder to wait, especially to find out that the person who is holding everything up already had transportation in the first place. That's a pisser, I tend to find. I'll be nice, I promise, I'll buy goods from solicitous youth who knock on my door, clinging to their one last desperate chance for a good, decent life that can be attained only if I buy a box of six caramel turtles for $12, even if I think that paying two bucks per candy item with enough wax in it to melt and pour on your bikini line is a little over the top, I mean, they're basically little chocolate candles without the wicks, and honestly, what kind of thanks is that for saving the life of delinquent youth? HARDLY ANY. I won't make faces or roll grapes in front of the people in the express lane with a full cart of food who are oblivious to the time they are sucking from the lives of the people behind them who only desire to purchase a fruit roll-up and a Mountain Dew.

I'm about to promise to be nice to my missing, dead husband if and when he is found alive when suddenly, from behind me, I hear a car pull up, and as I turn around, I can see it's him. He gets out of the car and waves.

"Where have you been?" I say as I run up to the porch, entirely relieved.

"At work," he says, giving me an odd look.

"You're almost an hour late!" I cry. "You are totally late!"

"It's only nine twenty-five," he says, opening the front door.

"No, it's not," I insist. "Don't try and trick me! Is that something your girlfriend told you to try?"

"What?" he says, looking at me. "It's nine twenty-five! Look at the clock!"

I look really hard, and no matter which way I squint my eyes, it still says the same thing. Big hand on the 9, little hand on 25. It's nine twenty-five. He is absolutely, perfectly, flawlessly on time.

Apparently, if all I really needed to know I learned in kindergarten, I wasn't paying close enough attention. Either that or Miss Brown, who I once threw up on because I forgot my snack, was simply not concerned with helping me avoid scenarios thirty years into the future in which I would accuse my spouse of cheating, alcoholism, and selfishness and, more horrifyingly, come dangerously close to making a sick promise to let city buses in ahead of me in a frantic yet paranoid moment because clearly I had not really, truly, and successfully learned how to tell time. Damn my codependency on digital clocks, and God help the six-year-olds of today with Velcro on their shoes, I scream in my head. In thirty years, I can just picture numerous corporate execs standing on train platforms, tears streaming down their faces, their mouths open in horror as they point to their feet, their shoelaces nearly liberated and unbound as they shriek, "CAN SOMEBODY HELP ME?"

"Why is my pillow and the dog's blanket on the couch?" my husband asks me.

"I was just getting ready to change your pillowcase," I reply, with a smile. "And just so you know, if a gang member comes to the door and asks you to buy candy for thirteen dollars, you hand him a can of spray paint and show him to the nearest wall."

Enough with the Love: Aberrant Tales of an Absolutely and Completely Normal Family (as Told to My Therapist)

Every March, I curse myself for my holiday spirit. That's typically when my husband and I will finally turn off the television set, finish off our frozen dinners, and do the nasty task we've been putting off for four months.

We take down the Christmas tree.

If it was really up to us, we would most likely leave it up all year-round and just replace it with another one after every Thanksgiving. Same with the lights trimming the eaves of our house, except we'd replace those only when they started to spark or catch things on fire.

We're that kind of people. Halfway folks. When it was time to repaint the exterior of the house last year, we took a good look at the twenty-eight window sashes and the eight peaks in our roof and decided that it was really only the front of our house that needed new paint. That's the part that everyone sees most.

I don't curse myself as much during the decoration removal as my husband does, and I understand that. With his hair filled with brown, curling pine needles and his hands scratched from the dried and dead trunk, he'll tow the tree through the house out to the backyard, mumbling, "You and your big ideas! This is the third dead Christmas tree we'll have in the backyard! Are you happy? We have enough old wood out there to raise a barn!"

"That's only enough for a teepee," I'll correct him.

It's at that point that I'll swear to myself, never again. I'll look at the petrified forest out there and shake my head. Not this year, I'll tell myself, I'm not getting sucked in. But slowly, ever so slowly, it happens. The transformation begins. I buy small presents, then big presents, then more big presents. Last year I even bought one for my boss, who I discovered had read all of my personal e-mail. I go to the supermarket with my husband's truck for weeks until I finally tell the cashier, "I need a pack of Camels, a book of stamps, a bag of ice, and . . . oh yeah, a tree. Got a twenty-footer?" When my husband finds the tree after my unsuccessful attempt to hide it or blend it into the decor, I insist that I'm just holding on to it for a friend. I buy wrapping paper and tape, and I found myself last Christmas making gift tags out of pieces of cork and a rubber stamp. In Target, I argued with a hefty, permed housewife who could have easily taken me down with one swipe of her paw over the last string of gold lights. *Gold lights?* Who am I, I thought, brushing the dirt from my skirt as I got up, Wayne Newton?

This year, at our Thanksgiving family dinner, I was feeling so determined that in between family fights, I actually got out the words "I don't think we should exchange gifts this year."

Everyone got quiet. My mother was first to speak.

"What the hell is wrong with you?" she shouted, hitting me with the dish towel she had posted over her shoulder. "Is that the way you want to celebrate Christmas? Like an animal? What should I make for Christmas dinner? Maybe we should kill a family pet and the rest of us will eat after it's your father's turn at the carcass? Answer me!"

I hadn't been in that much trouble since my friend forged my mom's signature on a deficiency notice in eleventh grade.

"I already bought your gift," my younger sister said before she burst into tears. "And it wasn't even on sale!"

"Well, if you don't want to get me anything, that's fine!" my other sister said with a glare. "But you're my sister . . . and I love you!"

"I love everybody," my nana piped in from the corner.

"Enough with the love! We don't talk like that in this house!" my mother shouted, and then turned to my sister. "You've been to Sedona too many goddamned times! And you," she said, turning back to me, "better get your ass back to church!"

"Everybody shut up or you're all getting life insurance policies for Christmas!" my father said, rising from his chair. The room hushed.

You have a BIG MOUTH, my husband mouthed silently to me.

"One Christmas Eve when I was a little boy," my father said, "we waited for my father to come home from work. Grandma had the Christmas Eve antipasta on the table, and everybody was excited to open their presents. It got dark. Still, Grandpa didn't come home. It got later, and later. Finally, Grandpa's boss came to the house and told us that the coal mine had collapsed, and Grandpa was trapped inside. We all started to cry. The men from the town worked all night, digging to try and rescue Grandpa, and as the sun came up on Christmas Day, they heard him calling from the mine. They pulled him to safety just as the whole mine collapsed and got sucked down into the ground. But Grandpa was safe, and that was the best present we could have had. We forgot all about our gifts until a couple of days later, we were so happy.

"That's when I understood what Christmas is about. It's about family, and being together. It's about being grateful that everyone you care about—yes, even *love*—is safe and healthy. So Laurie, if you don't feel that buying presents is a way that you want to celebrate Christmas, well, then, I'll break both your legs right now in front of everybody. Your sister paid full price!"

Oh yeah. Way more trouble than when I got expelled from journalism camp for drinking when I was a senior in high school. Only my arm was threatened then.

"I guess we're celebrating Christmas," my husband said on the way home. "But your dad was right. Christmas is about bigger things than taking down lights."

"Glad you said that," I said. "Especially because there are no coal mines in Brooklyn. Pull over! I see a twenty-two-footer in that Safeway parking lot!"

Jingle Hell

We all knew that Frank had way too much time on his hands.

All of the neighbors agreed, perhaps not in a ballot-casted community vote, but at one time or another, everyone on the block had taken notice, assessed the situation, and had decided that the ninety-pound man who lived across the street from me had spun madly out of control.

It was far beyond our control, anyway.

The first indication that something was seriously wrong on our street came on Thanksgiving Day several years ago, in the shape of eight full-size plywood reindeer, complete with leather reins and bold, brass jingle bells, all planted firmly in Frank's yard. Behind them glided a robust, gleaming Santa and his sleigh, which was bigger than any actual car that the neighbors owned.

My neighbor Mike sadly shook his head as he scratched his belly. "That's a man with trouble in his heart," he said to me, nodding to the holiday extravaganza across the street. "And trouble in his pants. Somebody in that house needs to get laid."

I had to agree. We all knew Frank didn't have any kids, and spent almost all of his spare time manicuring his already perfect lawn, which made the rest of the neighbors look really bad, especially because we had all moved into a white trash neighborhood specifically so we could spend our leisure time getting drunk and not installing sprinkler systems. Frank had no right trying to fancy up his yard; he was ruining our street, particularly when my next-door neighbors caught the Fancy Yard Fever from Frank and tried to gussy up their place during Christmas, too. The only problem with their improvement was that they were really poor, so they made all of their decorations out of used, broken things. I remember the most precious of which consisted of a huge five-pointed star made out of silver tinsel, held up on an easel and framed with a circle of tinsel around the outside. In short, they weren't too bright, since they had inadvertently propped up an enormous, shiny pentagram six feet from my house in a very sorry attempt to outdo Frank.

The next year was even worse. In addition to the Santa setup, Frank presented the street with a miniature Disneyland theme, including a Bambi, Thumper, all seven Dwarfs, and a terribly disfigured Dumbo that looked more like a sow than a circus elephant, which he nailed to the top of the tallest tree in his yard. That was also the year he set up a sound apparatus that blared out the Chipmunks and a twinkle-light system that required the expertise of an architect. It had become horribly apparent to all of us that Frank had redirected most, if not all, of his sexual energy away from his wife and into the direction of a jigsaw and sheets of lumber.

This was confirmed one afternoon when all of the neighbors came out to fake work on their yards so we could watch Frank fight with his wife as they were stringing up the lights and disaster struck. Frank's wife, it seemed, had handed him the wrong end of the extension cord, and in a fit of unleashed fury, he hurled it off the ladder and onto the ground, where it landed in front of her. She looked at the cord, then at him, and back to the cord again.

"Well, you can take that cord and plug it straight into your ass, Frank" was the only thing she said before she walked into the house. Frank got very nervous and started uttering mumbled phrases, although I did catch his comment that she "was only a woman, how could she know about man's work like this?"

On the heels of every disaster, tragedy naturally follows, and Frank's yard was no exception. One sunny December morning, everyone on my street woke up to Frank howling mournfully, and a brush of my bedroom curtains revealed a tortured man with his hands on his head, screaming for God over and over again in a crucial plea for compensation. A further brush revealed a hand-crafted and diligently loved set of reindeers now embellished overnight, by way of black spray paint, with a full set of impressive male genitalia.

That night, the Chipmunks did not sing. Frank had a plan to catch the reindeer marauders. I don't know what it was, but I know that it included a tennis racket and a bunch of rope, because that was what he hauled out into the carport as the sun was setting. When it got dark, he commandeered his post in a corner of the carport, sitting on a wooden stool with all of the lights off, a little man alone. I couldn't see him but I knew he was there because I could see the glow of his cigarette every time he took a drag. The Christmas King guarded his castle for six nights in a row until Christmas came, and he never caught anybody.

The years that followed brought the "Peanuts" characters to Frank's house, as well as the Simpsons, Frosty the Snowman, and an assorted gang of demonic elves that guarded the compound with steaming red eyes not unlike those of Jody, the demonic pig from *The Amityville Horror*.

An attempt to kidnap Snoopy was thwarted when one of Frank's stepsons came home drunk one night and grazed several of the vandals with his car as he attempted to turn into the driveway, although they still managed to escape. This time, a tennis racket wasn't going to be enough security for the yard, and Frank unabashedly and almost proudly told me of the network he had set up in the neighborhood. It included other seasonal decoration fanatics, CB radios, and guns. One guy was set up three blocks to the west and the other guy one block to the east. If a vandal was spotted, or even suspected, the network participants would signal to one another as to which direction the perp was heading, and if one was caught, Frank told me point-blank that he wouldn't hesitate to shoot.

The duration of that season, quite thankfully, was uneventful.

The next year, we could all tell that something big was brewing in the elf factory of Frank's backyard when sounds of saws, hammers, and sanders consumed our street for weeks. We held our breath for Thanksgiving Day, Frank's annual self-appointed unveiling date.

And we waited.

And waited.

And waited.

Thanksgiving Day came and went, blanketed with a bitter silence as our turkeys turned rancid.

Nothing was happening in Frank's yard, not a string of lights or a note of Christmas melodies. Something was very, very wrong. It felt dangerous.

It was impossible that he had had sex. His wife had left him during the summer.

Then, one night, I was napping when I heard it.

Tap tap tap.

Tap tap tap.

The tinkle of Frank's hammer.

I jumped out of bed, as I'm sure my neighbors did, and peered across the way to Frank's yard, but it was too dark. The sun had already gone down, and all I could see was a big, lumpy shape of something with a floating red light toward the bottom that must have been Frank. I was going to have to wait until morning. Frank, you see, was teasing us.

The next morning, the first thing I did, without even lighting a cigarette, was open the bedroom curtains to see the new creation.

It was bigger than anything I had ever seen on Frank's lawn before.

It was six feet tall.

It was a monolith.

It was wearing a Santa suit.

It was purple.

It was BARNEY.

Of course I screamed. The first thing I thought was that at nighttime, the thing was going to come alive, gallop across the street, and peek in my windows, mouthing that it loved me.

If Barney was the agent of Satan, as I believed him to be, that made Frank the devil, even if he did weigh less than me. My fear grew even more enormous when I remembered that I was having a Christmas party in a week, and if I knew my friends like I thought I did, Barney had better brush up on some tricks from hell or borrow my neighbor's pentagram for protection, because he didn't stand a chance against my guests, which, in turn, was going to put me in an ocean of boiling water with Frank.

Then a miracle happened.

Barney was shanghaied the night before my party. I couldn't believe my good luck. I was off the hook; I couldn't be implicated in Barney's abduction no matter what.

The night of my party, Frank hadn't even flickered the Christmas lights. The yard remained dark, black, and mourning.

My husband, under the influence of some foul though potent wassail, took a tribe of guests to the other side of the street to prove to them that I don't make this shit up. There they were, gawking and amazed at the finery, wondering aloud what kind of nut would put forth such a worthless effort, when a voice rang out from Frank's porch.

"GET OUTTA MY YARD."

They were in trouble. My husband knows that Frank has guns.

"We were just admiring your yard," he said. "How did you get rid of—I mean, what happened to the Barney?"

"WOULDN'T GET ANY CLOSER IF I WERE YOU," Frank warned. "I GOT TWO HUNDRED AND TWENTY VOLTS IN THIS YARD."

And he did.

The entire yard was laced with trip wire, starting at the Snoopy that Frank had placed in Barney's spot as a lure for when the bandits came back. The lawn, the Bambi, the Linus, the Bart, the elves, were as hot as the Chair when the switch is pulled—well, maybe not that hot, but pretty hot, hot enough to fry a little kid who could wander into Frank's Christmas Death Trap by mistake.

The boys got out of the yard and came straight back to the party.

The next day, I had to go over to Frank's to apologize for something else that happened that night. My friend Keith thought it would be fun to bring the British punk band, U.K. Subs, to my house, but by the time they got there, everyone had already gone home. The band didn't have anyone to entertain them, so they went outside and threw grapefruits at Frank's yard until Frank announced that he had his rifle cocked and that they were just moving targets to him.

"I probably would have just shot 'em in the legs," Frank assured me. "Good thing for them that they didn't come in this yard. Got enough volts running through here to knock a horse on its ass."

It was then that I noticed the newest addition to Frank's yard, a hand-crafted sign that was spiked right near the entryway.

FORGET THE DOG, it pronounced.

That was odd, I thought, forget the dog?

Forget the dog?

Then it all made sense.

I read the next line.

BEWARE OF THE OWNER.

Well.

Enough said.

The Dead Zone

The smell was nauseating. It enveloped nearly the entire back-yard, shooting into our nostrils the minute we opened the back door.

If you've ever smelled death, you're not likely to forget it, and can identify that hellish scent without a flicker of hesitation. That's exactly what I did when the initial whiff hit me and nearly knocked me on my ass.

It didn't help that it was 106 degrees outside, either. Hoping that I was wrong about its origins, I turned to my husband for confirmation. The look on his face should have told me what I needed to know, but I asked anyway.

"Do you smell that?" I asked, as he covered his mouth and his eyes rolled back in his head. "Do you think it could just be stagnant water?"

"Not unless there's a body floating in it," my husband responded. "I think it's that cat."

I was afraid he would say that, though it's not my cat, Pee Boy, aka Barnaby (who I'm convinced is being kept alive by dark, supernatural forces to torment me in my own personal hell), he was talking about. The previous Saturday, my neurotic dog, terrorizer of all things blind, crippled, or severely injured, sounded the alarm that something was horrifyingly amiss in the far corner of the yard. Being that my dog also barks at trash floating through our yard, occasional gusts of wind, and falling leaves, you could say that I wasn't exactly reaching for a rifle to confront any potential danger, and chalked up her terrorized yelps to a fallen branch or perhaps a mysterious and taunting pile of doody she didn't remember creating the hour before.

Finally, under the suspicion that if she didn't cease her belabored moans, one of my neighbors was certain to shoot her, I went out to bring her back indoors. When I reached the corner of the yard, however, I gasped and covered my mouth.

There was Miss Kitty, a feral cat who had lived underneath our house longer than we had lived in it. A tiny little black and orange calico, she wasn't exactly what you would call affectionate, though after three years, our relationship had blossomed to the point that she didn't run away anymore when we encountered each other.

Now, however, Miss Kitty was hissing and spitting at my relentless dog, batting at her with full claws. I saw that she was in pretty bad shape, covered in dirt and bits of grass, as she tried to drag herself away from my dog but wasn't strong enough to do so. It was pretty apparent that she had been hit by a car. I grabbed the dog and took her inside, but when I came back to the corner of the yard with some water, Miss Kitty was gone. I searched the yard, the barn, and the shed, but she had vanished. I hoped that she wasn't as hurt as I thought she was and had scrambled off someplace safe to recoup.

But when I hadn't seen her for a couple of days and we smelled that smell for the first time, I knew what had happened. Miss Kitty had run into the little Kitty Light, and had departed for a place where Happy Cat Vittles are served at every meal and there is a conspicuous absence of lunatic dogs that bark at their own feces.

Miss Kitty may have been finally at peace, but I sure wasn't. Following the trail of stink, it led me, by thicker concentrations, to the crawl space under the house directly beneath my bedroom.

"It's impossible," I said to my husband, who had turned a greenish sort of hue and was now breathing into a paper bag. "All of the vents have been blocked up. She couldn't have gotten in there."

I had blocked the vents as a precaution, since Miss Kitty was not the first inhabitant of the City of the Dead that existed beneath my floorboards. While we were replumbing the house, we removed the bathroom floor, only to find what we initially thought was a twelve-piece bucket of KFC lying in the dirt below. We actually had the nerve to giggle about it until both my husband and I realized, in the same moment, that the Family Combo Meal had a tail. And ears. And a place for eyes.

It was a Kitty Mummy, and sometimes, on hot, humid nights, my husband still has dreams that the Mummy is chasing after him on two little fried-chicken legs, holding a shovel and a Hefty bag.

Now that the catacombs had reopened for public use, my husband was convinced that the Curse of the Kitty Mummy had been unleashed and began noticing unusual whiffs of coleslaw and mashed potatoes and gravy. That night, just for fun, I put a biscuit on his pillow.

The next morning, I woke to find him dressed in rubber gloves, a dish towel wrapped around his nose and mouth, and a hoe in his hands.

"I'm taking care of this now. Miss Kitty has got to go," he said as he looked for a flashlight. "There's danger under there. I'm no fool; I'm not waiting until I suddenly find a Spork plunged into my calf!"

Outside, he dropped to his belly and removed the barricade from the vent opening. The stink wave hit me in one, solid push. With his flashlight, my husband examined the burial chamber, but then stood up and shook his head.

"I can't find her," he mumbled from beneath the dish towel. "She's not under there."

"She HAS to be!" I cried. "That's where the smell is coming from. You didn't see anything?"

My husband shook his head. "Only this," he said as he held up a pure white Spork, perfectly contained and sealed in its own little package.

I gasped.

Peace, You Stupid Asshole

I was going down big-time.

It all happened very slowly.

I felt the THUD as I hit the floor, facedown.

I felt the dust settle around me.

"Oh my God!" I heard my husband yell, standing in the bathroom not two feet away from me. "Are you all right?"

I have told him before NOT to try and communicate with me if it appears that I am in pain, because I cannot be responsible for what flies out of my mouth. I guess he just forgot.

"JESUS, I HATE YOU, YOU STUPID ASSHOLE!" is apparently what I replied.

Don't think I'm mean; he has that rule, too. I learned it one day after he was lying on the couch and our special-needs dog jumped up on him and inadvertently almost popped the family jewels like they were ripe little figs.

He suddenly looked as if he had inhaled a golf ball, staggered off the couch, threw a matchbook at the dog, uttered the words "KILL THE BAD THING," and then stumbled into the kitchen. I followed quickly behind in case I needed to get the bag of frozen peas for an ice pack, but as I turned the corner, I saw him squatting on the floor with his hands on his head, pulling out his hair.

Without turning his head, he growled, *"Don't look at me! Don't look at me!"* and continued to rock back and forth like Dustin Hoffman in *Rainman*. Sympathetically, I tried to feel his agony. I guessed that it came kind of close to the time that my husband's friend was drunk at a party and decided to show us how well she River-danced. At the precise time that we heard her ankle crack and she crumpled into a heap, her cigarette flew from her hand and burned a big, brown hole in my brand-new irregular Kate Spade purse that I got for ten dollars at a clearance center but pretended in my head that I paid full price for, making me superior and special. I'm not sure whose howls were louder, mine or the River-dancer with the splintered bones, but I learned at that moment that agony doesn't have to be physical to rip your elitist soul right out of your body.

So I understood, and just whispered, "Peas are in the freezer under the ten-pound brisket you were going to take on that camping trip and eat off of for six days but couldn't fit into your back-pack and is now costing us ten dollars a month to keep frozen," and tiptoed back into the living room to watch TV.

I am a *great* wife.

But as I was sprawled on the floor, facedown like a drunk, my husband wasn't being as understanding, even though he saw the whole thing and didn't even laugh, which I guess means he loves me.

I looked at my fingers. They were starting to swell.

"Peas!" I gasped as my husband stood there. "Peas!"

"Oh honey, don't worry about it!" he said as he came forward. "I knew you didn't mean it when you called me an asshole. Peace to you, too!"

"Get me the frozen peas before I pop your little figs like bubble wrap, ASSHOLE," I winced.

When my husband returned with green beans, two of my fingers—the swear one and the one in between it and the pinkie—had grown to both the size and color of bratwurst. I could bend both a little, so I knew they weren't broken, but probably sprained pretty bad.

"What did I trip over?" I asked, looking behind me.

"A sheet," my husband said simply, crouched down and holding the green beans on my hand. "I was doing laundry and I guess I forgot to put the dirty stuff back in the hamper. . . ."

I'm no fool. Opportunities like this happen once in a lifetime. I've wanted a maid for three years, and now that my husband had rendered my extremities useless, this was prime time to cash in.

"My WHOLE HAND is broken!" I cried, holding it up. "These hands are my livelihood! I type with these hands! I make my living with these ten instruments!"

"I thought you only typed with the two pointer fingers," my husband answered.

"I WAS LEARNING," I growled. "Yes, those are the *primary* typers, but I was beginning to incorporate other helper fingers on a one-by-one basis!"

"Do you want to go to the emergency room?" my husband asked, and I really did think about it, even if just for the drama.

"What's a doctor going to do?" I asked, mostly to myself. "He's going to put a splint on my finger and wrap it with tape, right?"

My husband nodded.

"Well, I ate a Fudgsicle last night so I have a stick, and we have tape," I said. "Pioneer women would have just bandaged their hand and gone back out to work the crops! I don't need a doctor! I'm from strong stock! What I really think we need to do is immediately call a maid service."

"First of all," he started, "the only strong thing about your stock is their New York accents. Second, pioneer women regularly died in childbirth and pulled rotten teeth out with their bare hands, but we don't live on the prairie in South Dakota. The hospital is right across the street. And third, if you think you can pick a crop right now, you can jiggle a dust rag."

"I was speaking in metaphors!" I protested. "Besides, *you* broke my finger! Why can't you put things away?"

"I broke your finger?" he questioned in a loud voice. "Why can't you watch where you're going?"

Then he gasped.

"You put that finger down," he said harshly. "Put that finger down!"

"I can't," I said as I smiled. "I have a feeling it's going to be like this for the next six weeks, or until I get a maid with ten more helper fingers."

My Mother, My Self, My God

How long is this going to take?" my mother said as she sat down at the table. "I'm missing a very good show on QVC by having lunch with you."

I took a deep breath.

This whole thing was my therapist's idea, not mine. Ever since my mom and I jointly planned the whole wedding shebang, things had been rather strained between us. A few months ago, while engrossed in a telephone conversation with her, we got into a disagreement that began because I hadn't returned a piece of Tupperware I borrowed. After we finally hung up on each other, she kept calling me back, over and over and over again. Finally, I became exasperated and just let the phone ring, because I didn't feel like fighting anymore.

Early, early, *early* the next morning, almost before the sun even rose, the doorbell rang. Then someone knocked. I finally got out of bed and answered the door. There was no one there. I stepped out onto the porch, and there, in *my front yard*, was my Nana and Pop Pop, peeking in my bedroom window.

"What are you doing?" I asked.

Nana, who was clutching her little Nana purse tight against her, was surprised. "Oh thank God," she said. "We were so worried."

"Worried about what?" I asked. "Why are you looking in my window?"

"Your mother sent us over," Nana explained. "You didn't answer the phone. She thought you . . ."

"What? She thought I . . . what?" I said, shaking my head.

"*You know,*" Nana said, waving one of her hands.

I still had no idea.

She leaned in closer. "*Died,*" she whispered.

I understood immediately.

"You mean she thought I killed myself," I answered.

"Well," Nana said as she shrugged slightly.

"You mean she thought I killed myself over *a piece of Tupperware* and then told you to come over and find my dead body?" I said again, a little stunned at the thought of my grandparents pointing through the glass of my bedroom window, asking each other, "Is that her or is it a pile of dirty laundry? Do you think that thing hanging from the ceiling fan is a body or a big cobweb? These windows are so filthy we can't see anything!"

So, in order for us to set things straight and to avoid having my grandparents sent on any more corpse-recovery missions, I invited my mom out for a nice lunch, even though it was courting danger. The last time we sat down and had a one-on-one talk, face-to-face, without a referee, I was nine and taking a bath when she opened the bathroom door and proceeded to set up a display that rivaled anything a Kimberly-Clark sales rep had access to. She had maxi pads, she had belts, she had a copy of *Are You There, God? It's Me, Margaret.* Then, as my bathwater began to form a thin layer of ice, she handed me some literature, told me to read it, take the quiz at the end, and then tell her my score. Right then and there I knew that the single most important piece of information I could take away from our mother-daughter talk that night was just how important it was to lock a bathroom door, especially if you don't feel like breaking out a window and running through your own backyard naked, looking very much like the girls you just saw in the graph labeled "Breast Buds" of the "You've Made a New Friend and She's Coming to Visit You Once a Month!" pamphlet. Still, that enlightenment could not compare with "the talk" my mother delivered to my youngest sister, Lisa, when she was about nine. Apparently, my mom had abandoned her suprise-attack method and actually cornered my sister, fully clothed, after she arrived home from school one day. She summoned Lisa to the kitchen table, where she had already set up her cigarettes, a cup of coffee, and ashtray, which had taken the place of Judy Blume books and the entire Kotex product line. She cleared her throat and looked sternly at Lisa.

"Girls," my mother said, "have eggs."

And then the phone rang, and it was my aunt Joanne, so my mother lit a cigarette, went into the next room, and left my sister sitting at the kitchen table. Lisa sat there while my mom talked to my aunt Joanne, while my mom made dinner, while we ate dinner, then as my mom did the dishes, and as my mom smoked a ciga- rette and watched Tony Orlando and Dawn on TV.

And that was it.

"'Girls have eggs,'" Lisa, now in her thirties, recounted to me several weeks ago. "That's all I got. I spent the next six months completely terrified that the next time I went to the bathroom, I was going to find a full dozen in my pants, or at least enough to make a quiche."

Honestly, I was dying to ask my mom about my eggs, but as soon as we sat down at our "pal" lunch, as my therapist called it, I knew it was prime time for her to bug me about the menu of things she lives to bug me about. Although some subjects change seasonally ("Do you still have that pimple on your neck or is it a hickey?" "Just when are you going to return my Tupperware?" "If you're planning on giving me perfume for Christmas, save your- self the trouble and give me the cash instead. I can get everything cheaper on QVC."), she also has a schedule of regular items.

These find their way into every conversation and consist of "When are you going to make an appointment for the gynecologist?" "Is your house clean or is it still filthy?" "You're not smoking, are you, even though I can smell it on you so don't lie?" and "When are you going to be in a better mood?"

"You don't need to borrow money, do you?" my mother began by asking, which is an alternate selection. "Is that why you asked me to lunch? A lunch that I have a psychic premonition I'm going to end up paying for."

"Here is my Visa card, Mom," I said, pulling it out of my wallet. "I am planning on using this to pay for your lunch, just as long as the total bill does not exceed fifteen dollars and eighty-one cents. For the tip, I have five dollars in rolled pennies that Nana forgot in my car after I took her to get a perm. It's not stealing, really; if she would have called a cab it would have cost her twice as much."

My mother rolled her eyes.

This is my mom. In those rolling eyes, I will never be an adult. Never. I have a mortgage. I have a husband. I kind of, sort of have a job. To my mom, however, I'm still the sixth-grader whom she made get undressed in a dressing room with an eighty-year-old bra saleswoman at Sears when my "lentils" (breast buds) started to become "pintos" (knockers). Honestly, there was nothing I could do about it then, and if it happened today, I'd still be helpless. According to my mother, child abuse wasn't illegal until the 1980s, so under the grandfather clause, she can still whip off her shoe and hit me with it at any given time without consequence.

Just to be on the safe side, I ordered a bowl of soup. I winced when my mother ordered the chicken salad, because with her iced tea, her share of the meal was already eating half of the remaining available credit.

"What's the matter?" she said, staring at me. "You made a face."

"I did not," I denied, completely lying.

"Yes, you did," she said. "I saw a face. I swear I saw a face."

"No face, Mom," I denied again. "No face. No face for my New Pal."

My mother sat there, just looking at me.

"What do you want to talk about?" she said with a stone face.

"I don't know," I said, shrugging. "What did you do today?"

"I watched QVC," she said. "I bought four things."

"Oh," I said, trying to think of something else. "What did you do yesterday?"

"I watched QVC," she answered. "I bought three things."

Then she just sat there, looking at me.

Our food was delivered to the table.

My mother poked at her salad with a fork.

"How's your husband who does the thing with the ice?" she said, taking a forkful of lunch. "Pass the salt."

"See? This is pal talk," I replied, slurping off my spoon. "This is good. Well, it finally happened. I had to ban him from making ice cubes. He only fills up the tray halfway with water, which doesn't really make ice *cubes*, it makes ice *disks*. Not only is it impossible for me to get my fingernail positioned correctly to lift up the disk, but it takes half a tray to fill up a glass. Would you pass the salt?"

"And you wonder why you have a broken finger. Why didn't we go to the Camelback Inn?" my mother asked. "This place is awful. Pass the salt. "

"Look," I said, holding it up. "It's all deformed and useless. It doesn't even look like a finger anymore. It's like a claw. Pass the salt."

"You get a real kick out of doing that, don't you?" my mother said, shaking her fork at me. "That's a sin, you know, sin you wear like it's a fur coat! Did you make an appointment for the gynecologist yet? Pass the salt."

"Well," I said quietly, "I have been having that . . . not-so-fresh feeling. . . ."

"I'm *eating*, for Christ's sake!" she said as she shot me a look. "No porno talk when I have food in my mouth, all right? That's disgusting."

"How's your blood pressure?" I replied. "I see a vein in your neck that's pulsing out the rhythm to 'La Vida Loca.' "

"How are you doing with the smoking?" she volleyed back at me as she pushed her plate away. "And don't tell me that you quit, because your head smells like a big round ashtray!"

"It's not me, Mom," I started, taking a big breath. "It's sitting in all of those AA meetings. Did *you* go to the gynecologist yet? Or are there no more eggs in the henhouse?"

"Get that picture out of your head!" she hissed as the waiter took our dishes. "You should be more worried about the fact that you haven't been to the dentist in two years! I'm amazed that you don't spit out little bullets of teeth when you talk. Your mouth is as clean as your house. Filthy!"

"I only have one good hand!" I protested, holding up my bandaged digit. "I can barely wipe myself!"

"Excuse me," the waiter butted in quietly. "Do you have another card, because," and then he whispered this part, "this one's been . . . 'used up.' "

"I should start my own hot line, like Jackie Stallone," my mother said wryly as she dug for her Visa. "I told you I had a vision."

"Read my mind now, Mom," I said.

She looked at me.

"I'm wearing flip-flops," she warned. "I can have them off faster than you can say, 'Mommy, don't hit me!' "

"Mo—" I started.

"Lay off the salt," she said, looking at me closely as she put her shoe back on. "It's not a vitamin, you know. Your face is all puffed up like a water balloon."

"I learned it by watching you, okay!" I replied. "Do you think maybe we could get some diuretics on QVC?"

"You can get *God* on QVC," my mother said. "Come over. I'll even put it on my credit card. Quit rubbing your arm. I didn't hit you that hard."

It Only Says That on the Box

kay, this is the deal," I said to Nana after we had each se-cured a grocery cart at her favorite food store. "You do what you need to, I'll do what I need to, and we'll meet back here at this spot in half an hour, you got that?"

Nana nodded.

"You sure you don't need me to stay with you?" I asked.

"Nah, I'm fine," Nana answered. "I took a Pepcid before we left the house."

"So you're fine now?" I asked.

"Yeah, I said, I took a Pepcid," she answered. "What's so hard to understand?"

"You know, you take Pepcid every time something is a little wrong with you," I said. "You use it like it's some sort of snake oil. You have a headache, you take a Pepcid. You have a stomachache, you take a Pepcid. You even made me give it to you when you broke your arm! It's really only for heartburn, you know."

"It just says that on the box," Nana replied. "It's like they say Windex is only for glass, but you can clean a stove with it, too, you know."

"Just so you know, if you take more than four Pepcids, we have to call poison control and get your stomach pumped," I relayed.

"It says that on the box, too. And the same goes for Windex."

"Don't aggravate me or I'll have to take another one," Nana said. "I'll see you in half an hour."

As she pushed off toward the produce aisle, I turned and went the opposite way. Because I had shopping of my own to do, I figured we could get the job done twice as fast if we each did our own thing. Besides, I figured Nana would be fine on her own in a grocery store; after all, her father had owned a grocery store and so had her husband, my Pop Pop. It should be second nature to her, or at least like being in her own environment.

I had already learned the hard way that it was best if Nana and I split up during our shopping adventure. That enlightenment was bestowed upon me during the last, panicked days of 1999, when the Y2K bug threatened to turn us all back into Ma and Pa Ingalls, reading books by firelight and churning I Can't Believe It's Not Butter by hand.

I had been trying to get Nana to stock up on food for months, but she responded with flailing hands and the phrase, "If I lived through the Big War, I'll be fine this time, too. Besides, how could I even catch the Y2K bug? I feel fine and I've never even touched a computer!"

Never mind that Nana spent the entire duration of the Big War in her apartment in Brooklyn with a grocery downstairs that delivered, but once she heard that Kathie Lee Gifford bought an extra can of pork 'n' beans, Nana was ready to build a bunker and asked me to take her shopping for provisions.

Who else qualified for such a duty to make sure Nana didn't starve to death? Surely not my mother, who balked at the idea that the possibility of a Y2K disaster could even remotely hinder twenty-four-hour broadcasts of QVC, let alone shut down every single Chinese restaurant within a three-mile radius of her home, and certainly not my sisters, who planned on sucking off my parents and their "stockpile" (six cans of tomato paste my mother bought before she retired from being "Your, Your Sisters', and Your Father's Slave" in 1998).

The mere thought of my family starving to death in the fresh months of 2000 was so horrifying I didn't even want to envision it, let alone be a part of it. I had nonperishable supplies for my husband, because much like a bear, I had been getting ready for that thing for a while. There was enough stored fat in my thighs to sustain me for two months each, and I had calculated that I could last through an entire winter season off my ass alone, which had gotten so large it had begun to touch the base of my neck.

In my opinion, it was survival of the fattest.

The rest of my family, however, had not taken such precautions. I had briefly imagined a scenario in which my sister with the perfect nails struggles with the manual can opener, trying to dig into a feast contained in the last Mighty Dog can. After decades of tragic attempts, she will finally be able to fit into the size-two purple Gloria Vanderbilt jeans she bought in the eighth grade, and she screams when the can slips and then she holds up the carnage.

"My last nail!" she cries in fright, sadly studying the half-moon-shaped chip.

"You gonna eat that?" my mother says wearily as she staggers into the kitchen. "I could make a nice stock out of that nail."

I loved my Nana too much to let her suffer in that kind of House of Horrors and eat body-part soup.

So one Sunday in December, I got ready to teach Nana how to survive on her own as I drove her to the supermarket.

"Now we're just going to get you some staples," I assured her. "Just in case."

"What do I need staples for?" she asked. "I have Scotch tape. I thought we were going to get food. Kathie Lee said to get food."

"Okay," I said patiently. "We'll get some of that, too."

I got a cart at the store and directed Nana to the canned goods.

"Did you see the cover of that magazine?" she gasped as we walked by the checkout aisles. " 'Kathie Lee Catches Hubby with Hooker!' Oh, what a lie!! I watch that show every day, and if it was true, Kathie Lee would have said something!"

"Look!" I exclaimed. "This is great! Tuna is on sale, four cans for a dollar! Let's get you ten!"

"Oh," Nana said quietly, shaking her head. "I don't care too much for that. It tastes so . . . fishy."

"Okay," I said softly. "How about chicken?"

"Don't be ridiculous, that kind is all chunks," Nana replied. "I can't make a cutlet out of that. Why don't I get some nice boneless breasts from the butcher?"

"You won't be able to cook it," I tried to explain. "Kathie Lee didn't mention that? We need to buy you everything already cooked in cans. Like these vegetables. How about some green beans?"

"That is disgusting!" Nana exclaimed. "You want me to eat like an animal? I'll tell you who eats cold green beans. Animals, that's who!"

"Okay," I sighed, looking up and down the aisle. "What about some applesauce?"

"Yeah, all right," she said, not sounding thrilled. "I can eat that. But only if it's on sale."

"Why, look, it is!" I lied. "Now how about some crackers? You can put the canned chicken on it."

"Nah," Nana said, shaking her head. "I like toast better. Make a nice little sandwich."

"Nana," I said calmly, "there's no toast in the New World."

"What am I, a prisoner of war that I can't have toast?" Nana said excitedly. "Crackers get stuck in my teeth! I hate crackers! They make my mouth pasty! Give me the toast and I'll buy the tuna! I think that's fair!"

"How are you going to make toast if there's no electricity?" I asked her, throwing the saltines in the cart. "If you can't use the toaster? There is no toast in the New World, Nana! There are CRACKERS!"

"You know what?" Nana said. "I don't want to live in a world without toast. I have it every morning with my coffee and Regis and Kathie Lee. A little coffee, a little toast, a little joy. Your mother is right! You're just all excited about this thing because you get to be Little Prairie Girl in Her House!"

"Little House on the Prairie, Nana," I snapped. "And if people were smart, they'd be watching reruns right about now, paying strict attention to how Ma cooked over an open flame!"

"You're living in a fantasy land," Nana continued, her four-foot-ten-inch frame turning red. "Because petticoats and sun bonnets are never coming back!"

"They said the same thing about corduroy and halter tops," I said as I turned down the drink aisle. "But on the way home I'll take you to Charlotte Russe to prove how easily history forgets. How many gallons of water do you want?"

"I told you I drink COFFEE!" she shot back.

"Okay, I guess we're done, then," I replied, looking into the cart. "You have enough here to last you through lunch on January first."

"No, no, no," Nana said. "I'm not done yet. Reach up there and get me six loaves of bread. I'll be prepared, all right. If I go home and start toasting now, I'll have enough to last me until next New Year's!"

So you see, after the Y2K shopping lesson, I figured it was wise to let Nana do her own thing in the grocery store, even if she did get a little lost and especially since the millennium experience left me with an anger I couldn't readily explain toward browned bread. And that's exactly what I was doing as I scanned the aisles for something to pick up for dinner on our most recent visit to the supermarket when I spotted Nana at the end of one of them, looking as if she was closely studying several packages of batteries.

I had already perused the frozen food section, the produce department, and the butcher counter and had moved on to the chip aisle, where I realized that nachos would certainly be classified under "hot meals" in any reputable cookbook and tossed a couple of bags in the cart. As I was about to secure a log of processed cheese food, I passed the battery aisle and saw Nana still standing there.

"Do you need help, Nana?" I called.

"Well, I don't know," she replied. "See, I thought my clock broke but your mother said I just needed a battery."

"Well, what kind do you need?"

"This kind," she said as she pulled a Baggie with a AAA battery in it from the cuff of her blouse sleeve. "This is the old, broken battery from the clock. Now, see, this one looks similar, but it's not the right kind. I've looked through every battery here and none of them are the right kind."

"I'm sure they must have a triple-A battery somewhere," I replied, then noticed that she did indeed have a new pack of AAA batteries in her hand. "Like those. The ones you have in your hand are the right kind."

Nana smiled wryly at me. "That's what they *want* you to think!" she said as she pointed a finger at me. "See, you fell for it! If you were me, they would have already stolen your money and you'd be stuck with the wrong batteries!"

"Who?" I tried to argue. "Who is 'they'?"

Nana looked at me like I had just full-on cut the cheese.

" 'They,' " she informed me, "is them! *Them!* You know . . . *the people!*"

"What people?" I said, shaking my head.

"THE PEOPLE!!!! Who do you think? The battery people!" she cried. "But they can't fool me! They don't expect you to bring your old battery with you, but I did. I can tell that these batteries are all wrong because my battery is the brand with a cross at one end and a line at the other. These batteries aren't even clock batteries, because they only have the cross! These are bum batteries!"

Quickly determining the pros and cons of an impromptu lecture about positive and negative charges and their role in the life of a AAA Duracel, I decided to take the easier route instead.

"Oh," I said to Nana, taking the batteries from her hand. "Why didn't you say they were the *Cross and Line* kind of batteries? Well, no wonder you can't find them. You can only buy them at the Cross and Line Clock Battery Store, but luckily, there's one right by my house. I'll bring you some tomorrow."

"Thank God, because this whole thing was giving me a head-ache," Nana said, shaking her head. "I may need to take another Pepcid."

"You are basically a flophouse and a pimp away from Pepcid rehab, you know that?" I informed Nana. "But I'm not ready to go yet. I still need to get some things."

"Oh, so do I," she replied. "The batteries were the first thing on my list."

I headed over to pick up some chocolate chip Eggo waffles for another piping-hot dinner and then realized that spray cheese in a can must have been hot at some point to make it so . . . sprayable, and as I turned down that aisle, that's when I saw it.

My Nana, my four-ten Nana, attempting to scale a wall of baked beans like Spiderman. Now, true, Nana was only about a quarter of an inch off the ground as she stood on the bottom shelf in a brazen attempt to grab a tin of clams three feet above her, but I really didn't see that. What I saw was my mother's open palm coming in straight toward my head with the words, "What the hell kind of idiot are you that you let Nana climb all over Safeway like a baboon? She can barely reach the conveyor belt at the checkout stand, let alone a tin of clams on the top shelf! And YOU KNOW HOW SHE LOVES LINGUINE AND CLAM SAUCE! She loves it more than toast!"

"NANA!" I shouted as I ran toward her. "What are you doing?"

"Oh, it's all right, I'm wearing my Easy Spirit shoes with the two-inch heels," Nana said as she turned to look at me. "Looks like a pump but feels like a sneaker. I thought I could reach the clams up there in them."

"Nana," I said sternly, "even with your tall shoes on, you're still a head shorter than the Lollipop Kids. To get to the top shelf, you don't need high heels, you'd need a jet pack."

I put the clams in Nana's basket, which was miraculously full considering it had been only eight minutes since I'd left her at the battery display, and despite the fact that I was convinced she had spent most of that time facing off to a can of pork 'n' beans.

"You've been busy," I said, motioning to Nana's cart. "You are one fast shopper!"

"I was basically *born* in a grocery store," Nana reminded me. "What can I say, except I think I pulled something when I jumped down from that shelf. Let's go home. I wish I had taken another Pepcid."

"Well, I'm not letting you out of my sight this time," I said, following Nana to a checkout stand. "I'm going to get a Sunday paper. Do you want one?"

"Goodness, no!" Nana said as she threw up her arms. "I just got rid of all the old papers that were piled up! You know your Pop Pop, he saved every bit of junk he ever set his eyes on! You wouldn't believe what I found in that stack of papers, papers that said, 'Japanese Bomb Pearl Harbor,' 'President Kennedy Shot,' 'Man Walks on Moon'! You know? That's not news! I already knew all of that! 'Nixon Resigns'! Who doesn't know that? I don't know who he thought was going to read all of those newspapers unless he met a caveman! You know, I threw out my back when I took all of those newspapers to the alley! I had to take TWO Pepcids!"

Stunned, I just looked at her as she began to load her groceries onto the conveyor belt. "You threw away 'Japanese Bomb Pearl Harbor' and 'Man Walks on Moon'?" I asked slowly.

"Yeah," Nana said. "You mean you didn't know that? It's true, I saw it. It was more like bouncing on the moon."

I was still shaking my head as I began to help Nana put the groceries on the conveyor belt, when I spied a bright pink box.

"Nana," I said. "Can you explain to me what an eighty-four-year-old woman like yourself would be doing with a jumbo variety pack of Tampax? And Biore nose strips?"

Nana looked into the cart and was just about to reach for a package of prophylactics when I grabbed her hand.

"Are those little gold chocolate coins?" she asked. "I don't remember buying them, but I love little gold chocolate coins!"

"There's my cart!" I heard a woman yell from behind us. "I went to get a can of soup and when I turned around, my cart had been replaced with one that had four packages of Pepcid in it! Can I have my cart back, please?"

"I'm very sorry," I said to the lady as I hurriedly shoved everything back in the stolen cart.

"What aisle did you get these on?" Nana said as she pointed to the little gold coins. "They're my favorite!"

"Would you be so kind," I mentioned to Nana's victim, "as to toss over one of those Pepcids? I think I could really use one right about now."

The Craft Toothbrush

There was something stinky stuck to the bottom of my shoe.

"Ewww!" my husband cried as he waved his hand in front of his face when I walked through the back door from the garden. "What have you been eating?"

"It's cat poop," I tried to explain.

"WHY?" he demanded. "You still have a whole year's supply of low-fat Pop Tarts in the pantry from Y2K!"

"I didn't *eat* it," I replied, lifting up my shoe. "I know that even king-size Tootsie Rolls don't come that big. I stepped on it in the garden."

I hobbled to the bathroom and pulled out my trusty craft toothbrush, which I keep in the part of the medicine cabinet near my deodorant and toothpaste. I flicked the bristles with my thumb, and, judging that they were still firm and stiff, decided that the craft toothbrush would be the perfect tool for the job.

I knelt in front of the toilet and did my gruesome task, scraping out all of the cat deposit that had firmly wedged itself in between most of the treads. Rinsing the now very soiled and very stinky toothbrush in the toilet water, I was almost done when my husband appeared in the doorway and after a moment screamed, "WHAT ARE YOU DOING?"

"I'm finishing my poop Pop Tart and am washing it down with a cool drink from the potty," I said. "What does it look like? I'm cleaning my shoe!"

"Perhaps I should rephrase that," my husband said as his face turned all red. "Perhaps I should say, what are you doing cleaning the poopy shoe with *my* toothbrush?!"

I paused for a moment. "Oh, shut up," I finally said. "This is not your toothbrush. It's my craft toothbrush!"

"THAT is *my* toothbrush!" he insisted. "That is *my* toothbrush!"

"It is not," I persisted. "This is the one I use for crafts!"

It really couldn't be his toothbrush, I said to myself. We both keep our toothbrushes in a little silver container on the other end of the medicine cabinet. Mine is blue, his is green, and my craft toothbrush is gray. Besides, I knew he was still angry from a little practical joke I had played on him earlier that morning. After he finally hoisted his carcass out of bed at 11 A.M., I heard him grunting around in the bedroom until he screamed, "Have you seen my sweatpants?"

"Yes," I called back, because that was indeed true. I had seen them.

"Do you know where they are?" he continued.

"Yes," I answered, because I did indeed know where they were. I heard him emit a big, deep, heavy sigh.

"Well," he said, sighing again, "Where are they?"

I didn't answer for a couple of seconds because I knew that would get him more aggravated. "I'm wearing them," I finally said.

"I want to wear them," I heard him proclaim.

"Fine," I said as I took them off and walked to the bedroom to relinquish them. He wore them all morning, and after he took a shower and got dressed, he never even noticed the dirty pair of my underwear I had slipped into one of the sweatpants legs until I was forced to point them out.

"Now let's imagine how this would play out in divorce court," he said, pondering the thought. "'You see, Judge, my wife accused me of having an affair when her friend left her panties inside our dryer, she broke her stupid finger when she tripped over the laundry and blamed it on me, and then, oh yes, she put a pair of her dirty underwear with the torn waistband inside my pants that I wore all day.' Not only would I get everything, I bet he'd sentence you to community service, too, just for being a menace."

So, as I held the poopy craft toothbrush in my hands over the toilet, it only made sense that he was trying to get back at me for my very funny panty joke. So I just kept scrubbing.

"STOP THAT!" he screamed.

"How can this really be your toothbrush?" I answered sharply. "This is my craft toothbrush! If this is really your toothbrush, where did I find it?"

"In the medicine cabinet," he said as he stared at me, "behind the deodorant."

I stopped scrubbing. "And what color is it?" I asked slowly.

"My toothbrush, the one I put in my mouth every day, is *gray*," he replied loudly.

I paused. "Oh," I said simply as I held the toothbrush out to him. "Then I suppose this *is* yours."

"What else have you done with it?" he demanded. "Cleaning toilets? Brushing the dog's teeth? Polishing your shoes? Because it's been tasting *funny* lately, and last week, my gums started to bleed!"

"No, no, no," I said as I shook my head. "I didn't do any of those things. I just used it to get some stains out of stuff, like my pants."

And to get paint off the cabinet I was refinishing, to get some stubborn stains out of my frying pan, and to brush the *cat's* teeth, but I wasn't even sure if that one counted, because the only thing that successfully made contact with the feline's fangs was the skin on the top of my hand.

"Now let's imagine how this would play out in criminal court," my husband said calmly. "I think fifteen to twenty years for attempted murder is fair."

"I will buy you another toothbrush," I offered, trying to make amends, but he just stomped to the bedroom, armed with a hand mirror, where he examined his swollen, puffy, scarlet-colored gums.

I got dressed, ran down to the store, and bought him a real fancy toothbrush that bends and everything. My husband never said another word about pressing charges, and neither did I.

Until I got undressed for bed that night, and a gray toothbrush with brown bristles fell out of the leg of my pants and onto the floor.

The Littlest Operative

My three-year-old nephew Nicholas came at me with three of them in his arms.

A fish. An elephant. A frog.

I shook my head.

So far, it had been a long afternoon. In a misguided effort to be the world's best rock-and-roll baby-sitter, I told my nephew we could do whatever he liked for the afternoon he was to be in my charge.

"Let's do what you think is the most fun in the whole world," I naively said.

And that, directly, is how we came to be at the mall.

So far, it was no dutch treat. I had shelled out for the pizza, for the ice cream, for the Mountain Dew that he said he wanted and then promptly changed his mind when he realized I had Pepsi, and for the $5.95 Mickey Mouse lollipop that was bigger than his head.

For the $9 rubber gorilla he spotted in the first toy store we entered.

"You can have one toy," I reminded him. "Are you sure this is it?"

He nodded vigorously, clutching the animal to his chest.

"I love him," Nicholas said. "I will hold him like a baby."

"Awwww," I thought.

This strategic maneuver, I later learned, was called "Arrow in the Heart."

It is a simple and easy tactic, yet startlingly effective, especially on those who are both simple-minded and eager to please, such as aunts and grandmothers. It is such a basic command it can be employed by those as young as six months old with stunning and profitable results. Rumor has it that a toddler in Jersey City once acquired the stock of an entire Disney store after cooing, "Snow White not as pretty as you, Gramma. You fairest of them all."

On Nicholas's lead, we entered the next store, and before I even realized what was happening—within four seconds of crossing the threshold—I was being told by a salesperson that she "could take me over here."

"Excuse me?" I said, trying to keep an eye on my nephew, who was busy pointing at a massive toy display and telling another child, "I have that. I have that. I have that. I have that."

"He said you were buying this for him," she said, showing me a Tarzan book and pointing to the expert thirty-pound manipulator. The master terrorist just looked up and smiled.

I had just witnessed the "Behind Your Back Stealth Bomber" tactic, one that is definitely beyond novice level. It requires movement at the speed of light, the ability to identify, secure, and successfully attack a target without being noticed. This exercise works well on those easily confused, mixing medication, or often considered "not the brightest star in the sky." It is only fair to mention that my nephew, in the care of his other aunt (also my sister), got a sixty-pound Winnie the Pooh this way that's bigger than my father.

"Now you have two toys," I said as I wheeled the stroller out of the store. "We've reached Aunt Laurie's limits, especially the plastic one with the hologram on it."

At the next store, Nicholas looked at me and threw up his hands.

"What this?" he said sternly. "This no toy store."

"I know." I smiled. "It's a grown-up store. I need to get something for me."

Honestly, I don't even know how it happened; the child was next to me the whole time, but suddenly there he was, cradling bath toys in the shape of a fish, an elephant, and a frog.

"When we came into this store I told you no toys, remember?" I reminded him gently as I approached the sales counter with a bottle of my favorite lotion in my hand. "You need to put them back."

Desperate times require desperate measures. Nicholas's face transformed into the look he gets every time he watches the part of the movie when Bambi finally understands that his mother has scampered into the light and that he is completely and utterly alone in the world. The look typically happens in slow motion, and it's actually a work of art produced in stages. His eyebrows drop at the same rate as his upper lip, his mouth opens and extends downward, his tiny jowls tremble, and then his face flushes with red-hot angst. It is the look of true, unspeakable horror.

I stood there for a moment, trying to think rationally, which is simply impossible when confronted by a three-year-old who's on the verge of exploding, and I have only enough cash left in my wallet to buy what he has in his hand or what I have in mine. At that moment, I finally understood why my mother started taking eight Tylenols a day when I was seven and just never stopped. Her liver probably looks like a fishing net, but what the hell. At least she never threw herself in front of a moving toy train.

"How about this," I said, crouching down to his height. "How about if you pick the one you like the best, and we'll get you that one?"

"But I can't do that," he said softly, shaking his head. "They're already *friends*."

"Be a big boy and pick two," I said firmly.

He looked up at me, and I saw something shiny. Escaping from his right eye was a large tear the size of a chocolate-malted Whopper, so big it reflected light. I even *saw* myself in it. It teetered on the ledge of his lower eyelashes for a moment or two, then suddenly tumbled off and plunged furiously down his face, leaving a streak of sadness on his little baby cheek.

Man, I didn't stand a chance. "Napalm" is a method reserved for only the most experienced, most brave, and most gutsy of preschoolers. It's not for sissies. Under ideal conditions, the store will be crowded, thus increasing the humiliation level for the adult when the child throws himself on the ground, beats his head against the floor, or begins knocking over end caps. Effective, immediate results with any victim, but works particularly well if victim has a migraine or really needs a cigarette. Preschooler can boost power to superhuman strength if he or she has consumed a Pepsi and lollipop within the last hour.

As I loaded Nicholas into his car seat, followed by the gorilla, the book, and the bath toys, he looked at me and smiled.

"Oh, Aunt Laurie," he said in his sweetest voice, "you make me so happy."

I covered my mouth, and felt a warm, wet Whopper fall from my own face.

"Why you crying?" he said, sitting up.

I laughed, and wiped away the tear trail.

"Payback!" I shouted.

You Make Me Sick

It wasn't the first sneeze that scared me. When I heard my husband sneeze a third, fourth, and fifth time from the living room, I still had no fear. It's a common occurrence in our house; if you touch anything, move anything, or sit on anything, a sneeze is eminent. Our little dog, who I believe sustained minor brain damage from spending too much time out in the sun when she was a puppy, refuses to come back indoors unless she has completely coated herself with a thick layer of dirt and dead grass. If you try to brush her or pat the dirt off her, it just makes more. As a result, I have enough dust on some bookshelves to plant seeds in.

I wasn't scared until my husband woke up the next day and shook me awake.

"Honey, I don't feel so good," he squeaked out. "My throat feels scratchy."

Ten minutes later, he came back into the bedroom and leaned over me.

"I think I coughed up my colon," he whimpered. "What does it look like to you?"

Then he stared at me and muttered the most horrendous words a husband can ever say to his wife.

"You know, I think I'm going to stay home today."

I will say right now that my husband is the nicest guy on the planet. I knew when I married him that I got the best deal on the market, although I never thought a guy like him would ever settle for a big bag of trouble like me.

But when he gets sick, King Cranky is born, and a wave of panic washes over me when he mentions staying home. I know all about the vows I took when we got married—for richer, for poorer, in sickness and in health—but the man I married changes just as soon as he's unable to breathe out of one nostril. He becomes a walking testament to misery, shuffling around the house with two little wads of tissue compacted in his nose, poking his congested head in my office every couple minutes and asking me questions.

"I heard the phone ring. Is it for me?"

"Is it time for my pill yet?"

"How much longer do you have to work?"

"Where's the dictionary? I want to look up 'tuberculosis.' "

"I'm lonely."

"Boy, you type loud. Every time you press a key, it's like a dagger going into my brain."

"What are the symptoms for the West Nile virus again?"

"I'm bored."

"How do you make soup from scratch?"

"If the instructions on the box of oatmeal say it should cook for one minute, how long is that in the microwave?"

With that in mind, and the fact that I had a deadline that day, I jumped out of bed, rushed to the bathroom, and dug like an animal through our medicine chest.

"Here's some stuff to make you feel better," I offered to his droopy eyes, his pink nose, his chapped upper lip.

He unscrewed the top of the bottle and popped a pill into his mouth. "What are . . . Derma Caps?" he said weakly, reading the label as he turned the bottle around.

I gasped. "Spit it out!" I snapped, holding my hand out. "Spit it out! That's medicine for the dog's dandruff!"

I ran back to the bathroom and dug some more. Stashed in a box I still hadn't unpacked from our move, I hit gold. There, at the bottom, I found a whole box of a cold remedy you mix with water and then drink. I remember taking that stuff the last time I was sick, and how I passed out and flew into hallucinations before the last mouthful went down.

"This medicine," I told my husband, plopping the two fizzling tablets in a mug of water, "is better than drinking a whole fifth by yourself."

He downed it in one swallow. Within fifteen minutes, he was asleep on the couch, twitching and batting at things. It was magic.

I went back to work, but I checked on him every now and then, and was even privy to some of his hallucinations.

"I'm going to make *her* eat Derma Caps," he mumbled from the couch. "And see if *she* likes it!"

"Hey, all of you sailors, get out of my house! Put your pants on! Where's my wife?"

"I told you, mister, I'm Nick Barkley and I'm the head of this ranch!"

As soon as I even suspected that he was beginning to regain consciousness, I mixed up another batch of cold stuff and poured it down his throat. I had drugged him so heavily he could have written the White Album all by himself. By nightfall, I had made my deadline successfully, and went into the living room to see how many things I could put up my husband's nose before he woke up.

I had a nickel in my hand when he shuddered awake, rubbed his eyes, and said, "Honey, you don't look so good."

"I had a rough day with the sailors," I replied. "Choo!"

"Oh no," my husband gasped. "You're getting sick!"

"I am not!" I protested. "Choo! Choo! Choo!"

"I can't handle this," he replied, handing me a tissue. "You get so cranky when you're sick!"

"I do not!" I said angrily, patting my nose with the Kleenex.

"Will you quit looking at me! Move over, hog! I want to lie down there!"

"Can I get you anything?" he asked kindly.

"Shut your pie hole!" I screeched. "Choo! You made me sick! Your voice goes through me like daggers! Get me some soup! But I want it from scratch!"

"I've got something a little better," he said, getting up from the couch, and in no less than five seconds, I heard the familiar sounds of *Plop! Plop! Fizz! Fizz!* coming from the kitchen.

Big Black Bastard

Something smelled. Something smelled bad.

It was there when I was watching TV, when I was working, when I was cooking, and when I woke up.

It seemed nearly to have a life of its own; it came and went at will, becoming overpowering at one moment and a second later, it would just disappear. After watching an episode of *Sightings*, I became terrified that I had opened a portal to another dimension in my house as a result of a sad and clumsy attempt to dabble in voodoo the last time I was fired. After downing the nearly crystallized remains of a Mudslide-mix bottle I found in a cabinet, I became convinced that I should retaliate in an attack of unprecedented horror. This seemed like an especially good idea since I had recently received a souvenir voodoo doll from my friend Jamie, who had just vacationed in New Orleans.

As I pondered the most obvious inflictions—the breaking of an arm, the loss of sexual competence, the procurement of massive, floppy man-breasts with nipples the size of coasters—I decided on a horror far superior to those afflictions, well, except for the man-boobs curse because I couldn't figure out how to express that action through the doll. Instead, I decided to stick a pin through the doll's head while chanting the most malignant song ever known to man, so it would run through my ex-boss's head in a never-ending loop for all eternity and slowly drive him mad.

"Oh, Mickey, you're so fine, you're so fine you blow my mind, hey Mickey! hey Mickey!" I sang as I got ready to push the pin into the doll's head, but as I commenced the first clapping solo, the pin tragically shot from my hand and vanished somewhere on the floor below. After searching for another, all I found was a bobby pin and a chopstick, and after several attempts with both objects, I gave up and just crank-called the asshole instead.

Still, I was afraid that my drunken foray into the shadowy world of sorcery had acted as some kind of welcome mat for a wandering incubus or homeless devil-imp when the foul stench began making appearances. After exploring all other options (lack of personal hygiene, misplaced rotting food, leprosy), I had no other explanation for the smell.

I was showing my husband where I had found demonic proof— a definite cold spot in the living room—when he looked at me with wide eyes.

"YES! With my psychic antennae, I'm sensing that you're dangerously close to the gates of hell!" my husband said, and then suddenly gasped and pointed to the ceiling. "Oh. Sorry, it's just a vent!"

"How was I supposed to know that you turned the cooler on!" I protested as I pushed away our cat, Barnaby, who had mistaken my leg for the arm of the couch and was trying to claw the meat from my bones. The cat, none too pleased with the apparent rejection, retaliated with a scratchy and full-mouthed "meow."

It took approximately two seconds for my husband and me to be hit by the wave of smelly horror that festered in our lungs with the pain of a thousand bee stings.

"It's Barnaby!" we both gasped as we looked at the cat, who had stink lines and waves of stench emanating from his smelly kitty mouth.

I had first tried to brush his teeth years ago, an event that didn't go very well and subsequently caused one of my ex-boyfriends to comment while holding my hand, "I can tell you've seen some hard times, sister, but I think it's really sexy that you found the will to stay alive. Did you use a piece of glass? Because those scars are totally gnarly."

In the course of his life, a very long and tumultuous twelve years, Barnaby has managed to destroy every new piece of furniture I've ever purchased by either urinating on it or slicing it open like a cadaver with his devil claws. As we all know, cat pee is the most dangerous liquid substance on earth.

I've tried to combat the damage and called several upholstery cleaners to remove the smell. The first place I called quoted me $100 to start, but also mentioned that it would depend on the size of the couch and the size of the animal.

"Excuse me?" I questioned. "What do you mean the size of the animal? It's a cat. A HOUSE CAT, not a panther."

Once, in a curious moment, I totaled the damage at nearly five thousand dollars in assorted demolished love seats, chairs, couches, pillows, and, naturally, my clothes. As a result, I've had to resort to the old Notaro family tradition of covering nearly every stick of furniture with plastic in the form of tarps, old shower curtains, and Hefty garbage bags. If I could find a Glade air freshener in the scent of "Meatball," it would be just like walking into Grandma Notaro's house.

Barnaby, however, has a great life, and I know he's very happy. He is currently dating my husband's shoe, a Birkenstock named "Left One," and we often catch him during conjugal visits with her. He's never gone hungry, has toys to play with, and as the Great Fearless Hunter has the death of nearly a dozen paper towels and one cricket attributed to his name.

I was sure that because of Barnaby's advanced age, our friendship would be quickly coming to a close, so imagine my shock when a friend informed me that her cat had just turned twenty. Eight more years of bearing tinkle and bloodshed was more than I could stand, but I was powerless.

That is, until the stench of Barnaby's jowls polluted the airspace around me, and I suddenly had a thought. When I was in high school, my friend Doug took his cat named Fluffy to the vet to get her teeth cleaned. Fluffy, as it happened, simply never came back.

"We should get Barnaby's teeth cleaned," I suddenly said through my pinched nose and covered mouth to my husband, who nodded in agreement.

"Sometimes," I added in a loud whisper, "when they're under anesthesia, they just . . . slip away."

Now, for all of you who are getting ready to write me a hate letter on Hello Kitty stationery about how mean I am and you really hope God strikes me barren, let's imagine this: You show me your favorite piece of furniture, and we'll have Barnaby relieve himself on it, repeatedly. Then we'll let you play with Barnaby, and I'll even give you a lift to the emergency room to get your skin graft.

As I got Barnaby ready for his vet appointment several days later, I lowered him into his carryall, patted his head, and smiled sweetly.

"Be a good boy," I reminded him as he tried to slash the flesh on my hand into skin ribbons. "Now don't bite anyone, because I don't have insurance to cover that. Don't pee, and if you see a bright, white light, run toward it. There's Whiskas and Pounce in the light, Barnaby! Run into the light as fast as you can!"

In one last giant effort before my husband placed the carryall in the car, Barnaby bared his teeth and hissed at me, shooting hot air from the sewer that was his mouth.

When I went to pick him up at the end of the day, I was ready to hear the tragic news. I had practiced looking up at the sky as I thought of something really sad, like if chocolate Twizzlers were suddenly discontinued, so my eyes would get watery. I practiced quickly covering my mouth and saying, "Oh my God! Not Barnaby! Why, Lord, why?!!!!!"

The receptionist greeted me kindly, and took a deep breath. "It was more complicated than we thought," she said. "He really didn't like us, and it was very difficult to administer the anesthesia."

That was my cue. I looked up at the ceiling, thought of a world without the chewy satisfaction of a chocolate Twizzler, and felt my tear ducts begin to swell.

"It didn't go exactly as planned," she continued. "And the doctor tried very, very hard to save his—"

My hand flew to my mouth. "Oh my God!" I squeaked. "Not Barnaby! Why, Lord, why?!!!"

The receptionist gave me a puzzled look. "Tried very, very hard to save his TEETH," she interrupted, "but he had to pull a bunch of them. That will be two hundred eighty-seven dollars and fifty cents, please, cash, check, or credit card."

I just stared at her as a tear quickly slid down my cheek.

Boys and Girlas

"Aunt Laurie," my nephew said to me as he tugged on the fanny of his Pull-Ups. "My diaper feels funny."

I looked up from my magazine as he played with a puzzle on the coffee table. "Did you do fluffies?" I asked, using my mother's designated term for "doody."

He shook his head. "It feels *funny*," he said again, this time tugging at his diaper from the front.

I didn't really know what to do. I was only the baby-sitter, and was watching my nephew for the afternoon while my sister was at a doctor's appointment getting an ultrasound of my nephew's not-yet-born sibling. It was that doctor's visit that would tell us whether I was going to have a new niece or another nephew, and personally, I was pulling for a double X, or "girla," according to my nephew.

It's not that I don't like boys; I'm just not equipped to deal with them. I was raised with my two sisters in a household that was 80 percent female; the only guy, my father, dealt with his den of she-wolves by retreating to his upstairs cave and staying there for thirty years. Family issues consisted of each of us growling, "Mom, she's wearing my shirt without my permission!" "Mom, she used my Love's Baby Soft without my permission!" and "Mom, I only gave her permission to wear my clogs on Tuesday, and today is Wednesday!"

So when my sister, pregnant with my first nephew, informed all of us that she was going to have a BOY, we looked at each other, completely perplexed, though my father finally came downstairs and grinned from ear to ear. It would have made more sense if she would have said, "They think it's a badger!" or "Looks like we're having a cuttlefish!" because then at least we could have identi-fied it, or pictured it in our heads. But a BOY?

A BOY? She *had* to be kidding.

"But there are no cute BOY clothes," I argued. "Not even in Baby Gap."

"I can think of only one way to do a boy's hair," my other sister said. "And that's down."

"We'll love this baby no matter what it is," my mother said, try-ing to comfort my pregnant sister. "Even if it is a BOY."

"Maybe we can make it gay," I offered.

At the time I was thirty, but my mother hit me anyway.

Then, the BOY was born, and I recognized how special he was the first time his pee hit my mother's cheek as she changed his diaper prematurely.

"Every time you pee on Grandma," I whispered in his baby ear, "Aunt Laurie will pay you ten *dollars*."

Watching my mother deal with my nephew's equipment was worth passing up a linen blue and white sailor dress at Baby Gap, and buying the overalls instead. She was shocked speechless and I believe consulted a priest the first time my nephew touched what my mother called "the wingding."

"He was in the bathtub, and he just grabbed it," my mother later whispered to me. "He kind of gazed off into the distance, and got this look on his face like he was in a fantasy land."

Admittedly, I have to say I wasn't much better at dealing with it, although I was able to identify his tools by the correct biological term, "wee-wee," or the more advanced "hinky-dink." Still, however, if I could avoid speaking about it or referring to it in passing conversation with my nephew, I would. But that would prove impossible the afternoon I baby-sat.

"Aunt Laurie," my nephew insisted again, yanking at his diaper, "my wee-wee is big."

"Do you have to go pee-pee?" I asked.

"No," he said adamantly, "it's BIG."

I sighed. Dear God, I said to myself, they certainly do start obsessing about this kind of thing at a young age. No wonder it's such a tremendous deal. Big, big, big. I decided simply to feed into his ego.

"Okay," I agreed. "Yep, it's big."

"Aunt LAURIE," he said, getting frustrated, "LOOK AT IT!"

And then, suddenly, my Idiot Veil lifted, and I understood what my nephew was telling me.

"It's BOTHERING ME!!!!" he added.

How did this ever, EVER fall into MY lap? Why was I chosen to explain the nature of men to my nephew? ME. ME!!!! The one who didn't know the difference between boys and girls until I was consumed by horror when my best friend (who had a little brother) educated me about the male biology as we played tether ball on the playground when I was ten. I was so stunned that when the ball came swinging around the pole it smacked me square in the head. That means I spent nearly a third of my life thinking that everybody has the same stuff down there. That fact alone disqualifies me from dispensing any information of this sort. To ANYBODY, especially an impressionable toddler.

But I had to come up with something, and something fast.

"That sometimes happens with hinky-dinks," I said. "It's okay. If you think about kittens, it will go away."

"But why?" he asked, which was not what I wanted to hear.

"Let's sing a song!" I suggested, and began clapping my hands. "This land is your land, this land is my land! From California to the New York Island!"

He was having none of it.

"WHY, Aunt Laurie?" he insisted.

I took a deep breath. "Well," I started. "I'm not a boy, so I don't really know, but it's nothing scary. Every little boy has a wee-wee that sometimes . . . bothers them."

"Like Scotty across the street and Baby Mitchell?" he asked. "Just boys, no girlas?"

"Exactly." I nodded.

Luckily, at that moment, his mother and father walked through the front door.

"Guess what?" my sister said to her son. "You're going to have a new little brother!"

My God, I thought to myself, I can't do this again. Not again. At least now, however, I'd be a little more prepared for the next "big wee-wee" talk, where there would be no song singing, no clapping of the hands, no conversations about *stuff*, only a mad dash to the nearest pet store to find the kitten corral.

Pissing Off the Pee Taker

As soon as the door closed behind me, I knew that there was no going back.

Standing alone in a strange bathroom with a cup in my hand, I was slightly horrified and a little excited at the same time. Finally, I thought, a test I can pass, and I didn't even have to ruin a pair of shoes by writing the answers on them!

Apparently, I was the last of any of my friends to comply with a mandatory drug test for potential employment, mainly because I've been unemployed the longest. As a precaution, many of them filled me in with warnings:

"You'd better be nice and not treat them like pee handlers, because if you don't, they'll drop a rock of crack cocaine in your cup and foil the test, which goes on your PERMANENT FBI REC-ORD."

"Do the wise thing and shave, because they come in with you and watch the whole time. No, I don't think you can use your religious beliefs as an excuse, because no one likes a hairy girl, devout or not."

"You're going to have to get naked, I mean really naked."

"Don't try to sneak stuff in by shoving it up your butt. They'll look up there, oh they certainly will."

"Are you serious? Really, you're not kidding me? Someone actually wants to hire you?"

So with those words of wisdom and three gallons of Diet Coke under my belt, so to speak, I went to the drug-testing lab/medical center confident that I was prepared.

When I walked in, I realized I was sadly mistaken. A teen mom-to-be sat by the door in a chair, breathing heavily in patterns; a man with what looked like a knife wound moaned from the adjoining room; and a band of hooligans grouped in the corner looked like they were there for the same reason I was, except they were holding papers that listed them as defendants.

I timidly walked up to the front desk and gave the receptionist my paperwork.

"I'm here to pee," I told her quietly.

"Please have a seat," she said with a smile. "We'll call you when we're ready."

I suspected "getting ready" entailed the plugging in of stadium-quality lights and warming up the anal probe. And I sincerely hoped they would hurry, because I had been holding it in all day for this, and my bladder felt as big and full as the uterus of the teen mom who was sitting next to me.

I tried to read a magazine, but I was already getting itchy from the marathon shaving session I had conducted earlier. In fact, I'd had so much work to do that I had to conduct the session in segments because I kept running out of hot water in the shower. As a result, my entire body was so follicle-free I looked like a newborn rat, though I could feel the rush of fresh growth commencing in the areas that I had cleared the forest from first. And frankly, it wasn't in places I felt I could scratch without having to explain myself in front of a judge.

I really had to go, and had already been sitting in the waiting room for twenty minutes. I looked at the teen mom, hoping that her water hadn't broken yet, so that if my bodily functions surpassed my own control, I could blame it on her.

"Laurie," the receptionist finally called, opening the door.

She led me down a hallway to an alcove where a rather large, stocky bald man was waiting for me.

"This is Arthur," she said. "He'll be conducting the test."

Arthur smiled at me. He looked like an anal-probe kinda guy.

I shivered, and felt my bladder crack.

"Wash your hands, but don't use any soap," Arthur instructed, motioning toward the sink.

"If I turn that thing on," I warned, knowing that the levee was about to break and drown all of us, "I'm very afraid that we're going to have to collect my sample from a wet/dry vac via the carpet. I drank more this morning than an insecure freshman at a little-sister rush."

He motioned again.

I had to comply, and did it as quickly as I could.

"Now," he said, handing me a plastic cup, "fill this up to thirty."

"Thirty?" I asked, not understanding what he meant. Thirty seconds, thirty droplets, thirty ounces?

"Thirty," he emphasized again, pointing to a thin line on the cup, which I guess was marked in milliliters. "If it's less than thirty, you'll have to come back."

I walked into the bathroom and waited for Arthur to follow, but he just stood there.

"Ready when you are," I said, taking a deep breath and unbuttoning my pants.

Arthur just looked at me. "I don't take bribes, ma'am," he informed me as he stepped forward and shut the door.

Great, I thought as I stood alone in the bathroom. I've pissed off the pee taker. Now he's going to put rock cocaine in my sample just to get back at me, and the only job I'll ever be able to get will be in a live show in Tijuana with a donkey as my partner, because they're always looking for junkie whores.

Quickly, I sat, positioned the cup, and I let the river roll. In fact, the river was rolling so productively I felt it was kind of a shame to stop and waste all of that perfectly good urine as I topped off the cup.

When I was done, I stood, buttoned up, and opened the bathroom door to Arthur waiting on the other side.

"I know you said you don't take bribes," I said with a grin as I placed the cup in his hands, "but I figured a three hundred percent tip couldn't hurt."

What Drugs Can Do to a Family

"Laurie," my sister's slow, cracked voice strained on the answering machine. "I have to confess something (cough, cough), and I hope you're not mad."

My husband looked at me as we listened to the message together. "She sounds . . . drunk," he said with a puzzled look.

"Close," I sighed. "I think she's high."

It seems as if my sister had been picking up my old habits by executing some DUIs—Dialing Under the Influence—and something pretty big was about to tumble out of her mouth.

"She's *wasted!*" my husband exclaimed. "Listen to that slur! She sounds like Tom Brokaw!"

It was true. She was totally bombed.

But honestly, it really wasn't her fault. She has the flu.

Almost everyone I know has the flu except me, because I've learned my lesson. Last year, I had the flu so bad it made me give up my favorite hobby of smoking, and that was about as much fun as running into an ex-boyfriend after you've gained roughly forty pounds. So this year, I did the wise thing and got a $10 flu shot at the grocery store because I have only one hobby left, and if this year's flu wiped away my desire to pick at my face, I seriously doubt that I would ever feel any kind of joy ever again. Personally,

I have to tell you it was the best ten bucks I ever spent, not count-ing the time I bought the Suck-and-Tuck-It girdle, which I got a couple of months ago instead of rejoining the gym.

Almost everyone in my family got bit by the virus: both sisters, my father, brother-in-law, and nephew. My youngest sister was probably hit the hardest. Seven months pregnant and casting the same-size shadow of a market umbrella, she not only had herself to take care of, she had her husband and her son to attend to.

I can't really speak about my brother-in-law, but when the male in my house gets sick, no human on Earth has known greater pain. And I'm talking about *me*.

With two males in my sister's house, her husband and three-year-old son—only *one* of whom was actually acting his age—I could only imagine the agony she was going through. Out of what I believe was more pity than actual medicinal purposes, my sis-ter's understanding obstetrician prescribed a bottle of cough medicine with minute traces of codeine to ease her suffering.

It did a little more than ease them. Unlike me, who spent the entirety of my baby-making years on a bar stool, my sister had no prior experience with prescription-strength pharmaceuticals. During my college days, there were some mornings that I sur-prised myself just by *waking up*. For my sister, however, a little bit of codeine was apparently enough vice that I half expected her to have changed her name to Jasmine and donned sparkly hot pants and clear platform shoes, and to introduce me to her new gold-toothed friend "Manny" the next time I saw her.

"I took my cough syrup and I'm feeling a little bit better (cough, cough)," my sister's voice said, confirming what I had suspected. "It's supposed to make me sleep, but it's just kind of making me think about some stuff, and I wanted to call you and confess something to you."

"This should be good," I said aloud. "I always had a feeling that letter wasn't really from David Cassidy saying that when I turned twelve he would date me and sing at my birthday party!"

"When you were in high school, Dad used to have Susan B. Anthony dollars in his top dresser drawer," the message continued, "and I remember one time (cough, cough, cough) they thought you were stealing them, and I don't know, maybe you were, but I was stealing them, too. Not many. A couple dollars at a time when I needed extra lunch money, but then I saw Ricki Lake or Jerry Springer today and these two girls were sleeping with the same guy, and I was thinking, you know, it wasn't very nice of me to let Laurie take the blame for that."

"Susan B. Anthony dollars?" I said to the machine. "I never took any dollars! There were *dollars*?"

"And, like I said," the message went on, "maybe you were taking money, and I tried to tell Mom and Dad one time, and they said, 'WE KNOW WHO'S BEEN TAKING THE MONEY!' And I just wanted to tell you that. And my doctor said I would be fine, *burp*, excuse me, as long as I don't get addicted to codeine. Okay? Bye."

"I never took any dollars!" I said as my husband eyed me suspiciously. "I didn't! I swear!"

"BEEP!" the machine emitted, signaling another message.

"Laurie," the new voice said, "this is Dad (cough, cough). I just talked to your sister, and I'm sorry for placing all the Susan B. Anthony blame on you."

"I didn't take them, Dad!" I cried. "It wasn't me!"

"But I just took some medicine and got to thinking," the machine persisted. "And I wanted to ask you what you knew about my bicentennial quarters."

My husband looked at me again.

"Uh-oh," I said as I just stood there.

You Have Already Been Preapproved
for a Decline

Here, Casey!" the woman on the commercial called out gently. "Here, boy!"

Casey, a puppy in the same commercial mere seconds before, was now a hobbling, geriatric dog who was not too far off from being sent to "live" on a "farm" in the "country."

My throat swelled, expanding painfully as if I had eaten a pretzel that had lodged itself there and then hit my face on the coffee table after losing consciousness. As I felt a wet little tear rush down my cheek, I sniffled, and then I heard it.

A faint, nearly inaudible chuckle from the other end of the couch.

"What?" I said somewhat angrily, shooting my husband a look as I wiped my nose.

"You're crying at a dog food commercial," he informed me as he laughed and shook his head. "I'll get you some Valium in case Hallmark or an insurance company has the next thirty-second spot!"

"I'm not freaking out," I protested. "I'm just a little sad. That dog was so old."

"Um, I hate to point out the obvious," he added, "but you're crying because you're experiencing an 'emotion.' Last night when

I told you I was going to bed, you said, 'I'll be there in a minute. I'm waiting for the weather report,' and the other day when we took your car to the store, you had a full tank of gas! You're getting old."

I wanted to argue, I wanted to deny the whole thing, but I didn't. I retreated into my office, sat down, and thought about it. Okay, so I've seen grandmothers on Jerry Springer who are my age, but so is Cindy Crawford!

Was it true? Was I past my prime? Were my salad days now just dried-up remnants of lettuce at the bottom of the bowl? Was there a little expiration stamp someplace on my body that says, "Best if used by 10/31/1999"? I had to know the truth, and I had been dreading this moment since I first read in *Seventeen* about the "pencil test." It was the ultimate detection device that would signal the time when I, too, would soon go to "live" on a "farm" in the "country."

Placing a yellow No. 2 under each boob, I stood back and waited. And waited. But the pencils didn't budge, they didn't fall, they didn't wiggle, even when I shimmied. They were adhered to me as if I had stuck them there with chewing gum or Polident.

I sighed and felt like crying again.

Rocks in a sock. Past my prime. So past my prime, in fact, that I could have leaned a little to the left and drafted an entire letter or signed a check to my doctor for hormone therapy. I was sure that if I lay down with my arms outstretched, I would feel each boob slide off my rib cage and settle in its rightful spot, my armpit, like a beer can in a cozy. I braced myself against the bathroom sink and sighed. When did this happen? How could I have not seen the symptoms?

My mind raced with excuses, but it was all there. In little flashes, my mind clicked from one scene to the next. In the last election, I voted for a *Republican*. A week ago, I watched the *Billboard* Music Awards and didn't know who anyone was. Standing in line behind a kid with a tattoo across his entire arm, my mother's voice popped into my head and snarled, "Now there's a wise investment. The only time it really pays off is when you're lying on a steel table in a morgue without a driver's license in your pocket." I don't understand the new commercials for Levi's. I saved $19.34 on groceries a couple of days ago by using coupons and a Fresh Value card. When my mother asked me what I wanted for Christmas, I replied that I wanted some moles removed. I just finished reading something that had an "Oprah's Book Club" sticker on the cover. I still have all of the lids from a set of Tupperware I bought *a year ago*. Under very bright fluorescent lights in a bathroom at Rubio's Baja Grill, I discovered that God likes to play funny tricks and that gray hairs aren't limited simply to your head.

But those things can be explained, I told myself, you can attribute all of that behavior to stress or improper prescription-drug use in combination with alcohol. To a possible chemical imbalance. A split personality. I probably just have a brain tumor. Radiation and psychoanalysis can fix all of that. There's hope, I struggled to believe. Maybe my boobs are just taking a nap!

I guess I always knew this day would come, but I just didn't expect it so soon. Did it happen one day when I realized that I was sitting at a KFC drive-through window, dressed in a sweatshirt and slippers, waiting for my order of Popcorn Chicken to come up? Or was it the moment I spotted a teenage couple holding hands and I had the overwhelming desire to scream, "Don't trust him! You're three bases away from becoming a statistic living in government-funded housing, honey!"

And if so, if I am maturing, what's next for me? Do I wake up one day and find my uterus nestled at my feet, next to my cat? When do I start sneezing and peeing at the same time? When do I get teeth that I can keep in a glass of water or pull out at parties? When do I start farting in the company of others because I believe if I can't hear it, they can't either? Now it's just a matter of time before I start calling my husband "Daddy," despite the fact that my reproductive parts have remained on standby alert for decades but have never been called in for active duty.

It can't be true, I thought. I am completely immature. I'm in a bathroom jumping around with writing instruments stuck to me.

But after I put my shirt back on and went outside to check the mail, it was all in front of me in black and white, and there was no more denying it. Waiting passively for me in the mailbox was a letter. A simple little letter telling me that I had already been approved for an unsecured Visa credit card.

I thought it was an act of God when I got my long-distance phone service reconnected. But an unsecured Visa? Could it be true? Have I really been paying my bills on time? It was worse than I thought. Just how old have I become?

I ran inside to tell my husband, who was walking toward me with arms outstretched.

"I'm sorry I called you 'old,' " he said, putting his arms around me. "I just get so frightened when I see you show any kind of emotion besides anger and hate. It's so unlike you!"

"It's okay," I said, hugging him back.

"When I saw the full tank of gas," he added, "I thought, 'What has this creature done with my wife?' "

"It wasn't me," I replied, hugging him harder. "Nana filled up the tank after we ran out of gas and had to push the car to a Mobil when I was taking her to get a perm! Oh honey, you must have been so scared!"

"What was that?" my husband yelled suddenly and pulled away, plugging his nose. "Man, give me a little warning before you blow on that trumpet, will you?"

"I don't know what you're talking about," I replied staunchly. "I didn't hear a thing."

Tiger Woods Doesn't Know
Where I Live

When my gardener called one day and asked if I wanted a winter lawn that year, I'll admit that I gushed as unabashedly as a Junior Leaguer over the thought of a diamond-anniversary tennis bracelet.

Did I? Did I? My mind screamed. The promise of a thick, lush carpet of emerald green stretched over my front yard when all of the other lawns in my high-desert neighborhood sported ferret brown was a dream too beautiful to resist. A lovely, velvety, jeweled lawn. It would be the pride of my street. The envy of my neighbors. And, if I could convince my husband to remove the tinfoil that lined the inside of his office window, our home might never be mistaken for Section 8 housing again! I just might have the prettiest lawn and house in the neighborhood.

I imagined it, my mind flashing to the sight of cars lined up two deep and a mile long, people coming from miles around to catch a glimpse of my majestic, flawless winter lawn. It was a dream I had waited for my whole life.

"A winter lawn will be a hundred dollars," my lawn guy said.

"You are high! Forget it!" I screeched right before I hung up.

A hundred dollars! One hundred dollars! For a patch of winter grass? My lawn guy had obviously spent too much time inhaling around fertilizers and chemical products or licking his fingers after he handled them, like a dog that eats antifreeze. A hundred dollars!

I mean, honestly, what do you really need to make a winter lawn? Manure, seed, water, and sunshine. That's it. Manure is a buck a bag, the water comes out of my hose, and sunshine is free until it bakes a big, bulbous carcinoma on your face and you have to pay for chemotherapy. And although I didn't know exactly how much seed was, I was sure it wouldn't be much.

I don't know if my lawn guy thought I sat at home all day, passing out hundred-dollar bills to people who would change a lightbulb for me or for someone to butter my toast, but I thought a hundred dollars was an awful lot just to distribute a bag of seed and then sprinkle cow turds over it. It's not like it takes a degree or a license or anything; you just basically need to be able to walk. It's essentially a menial task. Honestly, the only reason I had a gardener/lawn guy in the first place was because I learned far too late that my husband was far too lazy for my own good.

I will freely admit that I married for love and because it seemed like the next logical step after stalking him got a little boring. I did not marry for money, status, or for my own personal groundskeeper, although I am not ruling out that possibility for subequent marriages. I knew my husband wasn't bringing the assets of a manly assortment of Craftsman tools to the marriage; the man could barely work a flashlight. He would try to shine it on me when I hovered outside his bedroom windows at night, but it looked more like a strobe light, since the missing battery-chamber cover was replaced with a slice of Scotch tape. Instead, he brought a guitar, the strobe flashlight, and the complete works of Shakespeare, the sum of which is almost not even worth suing over. I married my husband because he is the nicest man in the world, and I am the meanest girl, which I thought might bring me extra bargaining points with God after I died and was negotiating my release from becoming Mrs. Satan.

However, had I known that he had such a developed aversion to yard work before we got hitched, I could have negotiated for far less obligatory time in the bedroom before I took those vows. Believe me, I've learned my lesson, however, because "Ability to Push a Mower Once a Week" is notched right up there at number two on my list for "Essential and Nonnegotiable Qualities for Laurie's Second Husband," sandwiched in between #1) Does Not Experience Cramps and the Need to Run to the Public Rest Room Every Time We Make a Purchase Over Ten Dollars and #3) Will Have Goals Over and Above What Programs He Wants to Watch on TV That Night.

But the seed for a winter lawn was planted, so to speak, and instead of giving up on my dream, I decided that I would embark on the project myself.

Once at the home improvement store, I stood on the grass-seed aisle perplexed. There were about fifteen different bags of grass seed, and I had no idea which one I needed. Then, as if a ray of light from the heavens above was sent to direct me in my quest, a man walked up beside me, and as he reached for a specific bag of grass, I saw the telltale sign: big, brown half-moons over each fingertip. He had dirt under his nails! A gardener! He certainly knew which seed to pick if his hands were all filthy! I marveled at my good luck, and as soon as the gardener left with his prized bag of perfect seed, I grabbed the next one in the stack and struggled to flop all fifty pounds of it into my cart. It left me breathless, sweaty, and with one leg numb all the way down to my ankle, but when I was done, I had seed in my cart and I was one step closer to a winter lawn.

I pushed the cart over to the manure aisle, but since I really felt no need to be as choosy about feces, I selected the cheapest brand and loaded four bags on top of the seed. Then I headed toward the cashier, my cart piled high with one hundred pounds of neighbor envy.

The lady manning the register was none too pleased to see me.

She looked at the goods towering in my cart, took a deep breath, and rolled her eyes.

"You know I'm going to have to unload all of those bags of manure to get to the UPC code on the seed," she said, just so she could be confident that I knew how grossly I was inconveniencing her.

"Oh, that's okay," I said cheerfully, deciding to play along. "You just go for it! I don't mind one bit."

She looked at me, sneered, and then lifted all four bags out and onto the counter, although the last one gave her a little tug-of-war when it got snagged on the bottom of the fold-up seat, and she gladly took her pent-up vengeance and job dissatisfaction out on it.

I just stood there and smiled.

"The manure is two-fifty a bag," she said as she scanned each bag, and I was about to complain about the inordinate price when I heard the register beep with one more scan and the cashier continued, "And the seed is sixty dollars. It's specially engineered for golf courses. Will this be on your Visa?"

As the cashier piled all of the manure bags back on top of the seed, I was too stunned to say anything. I really wasn't sure what to do. I couldn't put the seed back and grab another bag. I knew that I probably had only one more good lift in me—and that was to put the bag of seed into the car—before I damaged my spinal cord so badly that I went numb from the waist down, although I was sure my husband wouldn't notice the difference. And frankly, I was just glad that he wasn't there to tell me he was going to have to poop when I pulled out that credit card.

So I paid for the seed and manure, which, with tax, came to an amazing total of $74.69, and I began pushing the cart out to my car. And I started to get mad. And then I got madder. And then I got madder. And madder, and madder, and madder. By the time I was at my car, I was fuming.

Sixty dollars for grass seed! *Sixty dollars!* For golf course grass!

Who's going to be walking on my grass, Tiger Woods? Tiger Woods is *never* going to come and see my grass! I don't need golf course grass, I just need something green to make my neighbors jealous! *Sixty dollars?*

The more I kept thinking about it, the angrier I became, and as I was unlocking the back door of my car, I apparently began vocalizing my dissatisfaction. I'm sure I noticed that people in the parking lot were turning around to look at me, but I didn't exactly care. In fact, I didn't care at all, especially when I lifted the second bag of manure into the car, the same bag that had fought valiantly with the cashier, and the moment it made contact with the upholstery, it spilled wide open, belching a huge, black dookie flow all over the back of my car.

"Goddamnit!" I yelled. "*Goddamnit!* There is shit in my car! There is *a ton* of shit in my car! It's like I lined six bulls up back here, poised their asses over the backseat, and fed them Ex-Lax! Jesus Christ! Goddamnit! *Goddamnit!*"

Well, apparently my outburst was enough for some housewife to dig her cell phone out of her purse and call the store's managers, or maybe I had attracted that kind of attention on my own, I don't know, but suddenly before me were two guys wearing back braces and the home improvement store's aprons.

"Can we help you with something?" the taller one asked. "It seems like you're having trouble."

That little question was the exact provocation I needed to unleash, and I am unashamed to say that I completely lost my shit. "Do you know how much this bag of grass seed cost me?" I said as I whipped around to face them. "Sixty dollars! *Sixty dollars!* How can you charge people sixty dollars for grass seed and not even have a sign up that says it's rich people's grass? How can you even get away with that, it's like false advertising? Which is illegal, I'll have you know! It *is illegal!* It is *against the law!* You know what I think? I think everyone in that garden department is licking their fingers after they handle chemicals, that's what I think, because you're all high! You have to be high to charge sixty dollars for grass seed! That's sixty dollars! *Sixty dollars!* And now look at this! That cashier sabotaged this bag to leak cow doody all over the back of my car. How am I going to clean that up? Can you smell that? *Can you smell that?* It smells like a 4-H parade in my car! I will never be able to get that smell out—it will cost me *another* sixty bucks to do that!"

And finally, after I got all of that out, after I had purged my anger, I just took a deep breath as the two home improvement store guys stared at me and I stared at them for a long, long, long time.

Finally, one of them broke the silence and cleared his throat.

"Um," he said, pointing up toward his eyebrow, "you have poop on your face."

All I could do was look at him.

Yes, I then nodded, I was sure I did have poop on my face, and I just kept nodding.

"Do you really need golf course grass?" the other guy in the apron asked.

"No," I barely croaked as I shook my head. "I don't even know Tiger Woods, there's no reason for him to come to my house."

"Okay," he replied in a gentle tone. "Then why don't I take this back to the store, exchange it for the bag of seed you do need, and get you a refund."

"Thank you," I squeaked. "I only wanted a winter lawn."

"I know, I know," the other guy said softly, as he took a paper napkin out of his pocket and handed it to me, again pointing to his head.

As I drove out of the home improvement store parking lot with the right bag of seventeen-dollar seed and a mostly poop-free head, I realized I had learned a great lesson.

If my gardener offered to change a lightbulb in my house for a hundred dollars, I was sure as shit going to give it to him.

I Think Someone Forgot
About My Needs

I just about froze when I saw on CNN that some stupid scientists in San Francisco have developed an experimental vaccine designed to fight Alzheimer's disease, and not only does it appear to be safe, but "a significant proportion of the patients were able to demonstrate an immune response" to the disease.

Great. Just great. I know you're going to think I'm mean, but I was *really counting* on an appearance from Alzheimer's in the golden years of my husband's life so that I could finally RELAX.

Sure, I'm totally happy that the vaccine will help everybody else in the world who may have gotten Alzheimer's later in life, but man, that was going to be my time to SHINE. I mean, my husband pretends to have selective touches of Alzheimer's now so that he may lead a resort-style life, but I just kept thinking, "You just wait until you REALLY don't know what your name is and we'll see who lays on the couch all day watching a *Law and Order* marathon THEN."

I had it all worked out. As soon as his memory started to slip and he started calling everyone "Mommy," out would come the tails and white gloves and they would go on my other half. "Your mommy traded you for a two-liter of RC Cola and a bag of Fun-yons," I'd get to say to him. "You're a butler now and you have fifty years' worth of trash-taking-out to catch up on! Grab that Hefty and chop, chop!"

You see, the day after our wedding, the man turned feral. As if he were a wolf-child just emerging from the forest, I had to reeducate him in the methods of subsistence as he barely clung to life, exclaiming, "What that big thing?" when pointing to the washing machine and howling in terror while retreating into a fetal position when I turned the vacuum on. I once found him wandering the house rubbing his chin and wondering aloud, "If I was a fork, where would I be?" In 1998, he started to paint the house, got half of the eave done, and then claimed that he saw a bright light and an angel told him to come back down. On another occasion, he actually did attempt to wash some dishes, but that little miracle was interrupted when he stopped to call 911 because he thought the shriveled skin on his hand meant that it was about to fall off.

Oh yeah. I had a list of projects I was saving for when the hallowed day arrived, including building a second-story bedroom-suite addition for me and "Go to the store, I have a craving for chocolate Twizzlers!" errands. Paint would never peel from my house again, because if my husband didn't remember who he was, how could he remember that he was afraid of heights? If he couldn't recall that the lawn mower was his enemy, I could reintroduce them as longtime friends.

See, Alzheimer's was going to be my last chance, because all other attempts at house-training him have failed. We're talking about a man who took down the Christmas lights with *big scissors*, remember, a man who would rather live in the dark like a bat for sustained periods of time than change a lightbulb, and a man who could not locate the alley if he had a sled and a team of dogs to lead him there. I had all kinds of plans and now they're all RUINED. I was finally going to get some work out of him, work I have been OWED!! With his memory wiped out, it would have been like programming a robot from scratch; I would have

had a clean slate with which to work! NOW all I have is a dirty
slate with more hair falling off him and more of a mess to
clean up!

Well, on second thought, maybe it's ME who deserves to forget
everything.

Queen Bee

BZZZZZZZZZ.

Bzzzzzz. Bzzzzzz.

The noise was driving me crazy. It had begun earlier in the morning in my office, and at first I thought I was having a stroke or that I was finally hearing the voices I had been waiting so long for. But after I entered the kitchen to light a cigarette off the stove, I noticed that the noise had stopped.

I returned to my office, and at first, all was quiet. I worked a little, made a phone call, then:

BZZZZZZZ. Bzzz. Bzz.

Investigating, I followed the sound and came to the window, where the noise was loudest. It was coming from behind the curtains, and when I lifted them I saw the culprit.

A big, black bee, trying to get back outside. Although I felt sorry for it—it must be frustrating not to understand the properties of a simple pane of glass—my natural instinct was to kill it. The last thing I needed was something the size of an OB tampon zooming around my head, trying to poke at me. Only the week before, I had a Conflict With Nature after I came in the house from watering the grass and something caught my eye. A mass, which was brown and the length of my hand, had attached itself to my T-shirt, right on my left boob, and it was moving. I became paralyzed and couldn't do anything but emit noises, which sounded like this— *WOOOOO! WOOO! WOOO! WOOO!*—and meant "Somebody help me! There's a bat on me! There's a bat on me!"

Sensing my danger, my husband ran in the kitchen after five minutes and pointed at the boob, his mouth dropping. Instead of swatting at the creature before it bit me and gave me rabies or laid eggs in my skin, he took me by the shoulders and walked me back outside. Protesting, I shook my head but he continued, remaining calm.

"It's okay," he said slowly. "Just get back outside."

"WOOOO!! WOO! WOO! WOOOOO!" I said, but I meant "Get this thing off me, you idiot! NOW! I know it's a bat! Hurry! It's giving me the hantavirus!"

As soon as we reached the porch, he swatted at me repeatedly until the thing came off and flew away.

"That bat was trying to suckle me!" I finally said after I caught my breath.

"That's funny," my husband said, going back inside. "That bat sure looked like a butterfly to me."

So following my husband's butterfly example (he's reading a book on Buddhism and he's not going to kill anything anymore), I found a cup and a piece of paper, scooped up the bee, and freed it outside, figuring the bee, like the butterfly, had followed me after I had watered the yard. I felt good about it until the next day when I heard BZZZZ. Bzzz. Bzzz from the window.

I gathered the cup and paper, and reliberated another captive bee.

I began to think it was odd that two bees had found their way into my office, but figured that sometimes bees zoom in the house when a door is opened, much like flies.

But the bee came back. Again. And again. And again.

For nearly two weeks, a bee would squat in my office until I found and captured it, and sometimes, while trying to get to the bee, I'd find a couple of dead ones, too.

I was starting to get scared. I mean *really* scared. Where were all of these bees coming from? Why did they like my office so much? Why were they all big and black?

I decided to eliminate all noise in the house, so when one came in, I could hear it and isolate it right away. I began to listen to the walls, and that's the way my husband found me one day when he came home from work.

"What are you doing?" he said, looking at me with my ear against the wall in my office.

"Shhh!" I said in a whisper. "Bees don't like noise!"

"Are they talking to you in the walls, honey?" he whispered back. "Are they asking you to be their queen?"

"Shut up," I shot back. "Killer bees!"

"Don't be ridiculous," he said. "They only attack old people in Apache Junction that try to light them on fire."

"I'm serious," I added. "I'm afraid we'll wake up one day and our bed will have turned into a honeycomb! I can't wash that out of the sheets! They're Polo!"

"You know, you've been acting very strange since the butterfly attack," he said calmly. "You keep seeing all of these bees, but I haven't seen one. Where are they?"

"I've been freeing them!" I exclaimed. "Because of Buddha!"

"You're not Buddhist, you're Catholic," my husband said. "You people will kill anything. Remember the Inquisition!"

Just then, I heard it. BZZZZ. Bzz. Bzzz.

"You've aggravated them!" I cried. "They're coming! Put a wet towel on your head!"

It was too late. The buzzing became louder and louder above us, until it almost echoed like the inside of a tin can. We both looked up at the ceiling, just in time to see a single bee emerge through a remnant of an old metal stovepipe that goes up into the roof that I forgot was there. The bee floated around the room for a second and then headed straight for the window.

"Well, there's your swarm," my husband said. "I don't think we'll need a blowtorch, though. Masking tape ought to do it."

I captured the new bee, freed it, and then taped up the hole.

I was finally safe from nature, I thought, and breathed a sigh of relief.

Somewhere, from the other end of the house, I heard a slight squeaky noise.

Chee-chee. Chee-chee.

Crickets.

Thirty-fffff

Y ou'll never believe this," my husband said as he stood in the doorway of the bathroom, looking down on me. "You know that woman I hate in my English class? The one with the continental shelf for a rear end who insists on broadcasting the details of her gory sex life in public?"

"The one who came to the class potluck with her three filthy kids who then touched every single roll and helped themselves to the cold-cut platter by using their hepatitis-contaminated fingers?" I asked, nodding. "The woman who had upper arms big as hams?"

"YES!!" my husband continued. "Well, it was her birthday today, so she brought in cupcakes. Someone asked her how old she was, and guess what?"

"What?" I played along.

"She said she was thirty-four!" he said, a look of amazement spreading across his face. "Thirty-four! So I said to the guy next to me, 'My wife is going to be thirty-four, and *she* doesn't look like that!' "

"OH MY GOD!" I yelled, standing up. "Don't go around *telling* people that! I am not going to be thirty-four, I'm going to be thirty-three."

He looked at me as if I had just said, "Look at this pretty little vase I made today from my own doody."

"You're thirty-three *now*," he said slowly. "And on your next birthday, which is the week after next, you'll then be *thirty-four*."

I did not believe him, and I continued to argue until he found a pen and paper and wrote, right in front of me, that the current year minus the year of my birth equaled thirty-four.

I'm not good at math, but my husband actually balances his checkbook, so he's more familiar with it than I.

I didn't know what to say. I *couldn't* say anything, although I was on the verge of freaking out. I had spent the entire year not only thinking—but believing—that I was thirty-two going on thirty-three. And it's not that thirty-four is old, because it's not, it's just that thirty-five is right next door, even though it has the altogether different zip code of Adult Land. It's a whole new category on surveys. I was shortly moving from the "24 to 34" group to "35 to death or life support."

Just like that, my days of carefree, reckless youth were suddenly behind me, shattering any hopes I now had of becoming a child prodigy, a girl wonder, or even a daytime television ingenue. How could this be? Beyond thirty-three was a whole realm of things I was not ready for. I might have to start acting my age, and I didn't have the slightest idea how to do that except I was pretty sure it involved eating something other than Cocoa Puffs for dinner and wearing clean clothes. I am still a child. I am basically an infant. Last week I ate a complete can of spray cheese in one, single day, solid proof that I am still incredibly immature. I always thought when it was time to grow up, I would just slip into my adult skin and be happy with it, but it didn't happen that way. I never got it in the mail.

When my mother was thirty-four, she drove a Country Squire station wagon and I was in high school. Me with a child, let alone one who survived into adolescence? I could drive a station wagon, sure, although chances were good to unbeatable that there'd be an occupied car seat riding on the roof of it.

What may be considered still somewhat "cute" or "wacky" at thirty-three—things like tucking your skirt into your panty hose and walking around like that for an entire day, eating a whole bag of chocolate Twizzlers in one sitting, and sticking your tongue out at a nasty driver who took your parking space—are no longer considered "cute" or "wacky" but now fall under the category of "functionally retarded" and "assigned a caseworker."

What's worse is that I only had a few days to get accustomed to this, due to my rapidly approaching birthday. It was impossible, I thought; how am I supposed to grow up in a little over a week?

"Oh my God, I'm really going to be thirty-fffff . . ." I muttered to myself, unable to even say the word.

I had, however, a partner in this crisis; Jamie, my best friend since third grade, was born exactly a week before I was. I ran for the phone.

"Hi, it's me," I said when she picked up. "Are you busy?"

"No, I'm just watching *Sigmund and the Sea Monsters*," she answered.

"Do you know we're going to be thirty-fffff . . . ?" I whimpered. "I just found out."

"You *are* bad at math," she said.

"You knew?" I asked.

"I'm a microbiologist," she explained. "It's important when you're trying to find a cure for cancer that you know how to subtract."

"See? At least you have a career," I argued, feeling even more depressed. "When you answer the phone at work, you say, 'Molecular Genetics, this is Jamie,' and when I answer the phone, all I get to say is 'Hi.' I don't feel like a grown-up, do you?"

"No, I'm a kid in a lab coat," she admitted. "I keep having stress dreams that I get exposed at work and my boss calls me 'duplicitous,' and I don't even know if that's a *word*."

"I can't be thirty-fffff . . ." I whined. "I ate an entire can of spray cheese yesterday by myself, except for the stuff that I sprayed into the dog's mouth."

"People stared at me all day yesterday, and I thought it was because I looked especially beautiful," she said. "But when I got home, I realized it was because a button had popped off my shirt and my left boob had come out to get some air."

Then we both giggled.

"I don't want to be thirty-fffff . . . ," I sniveled. "What are we going to do?"

"We're going to stay thirty-three," she said firmly.

"Can we do that?" I asked.

"Of course we can," she answered. "If we don't feel thirty-fffff, let's not be thirty-fffff. When the time is right, then we'll move on. But I have to go now. My Cap'n Crunch is getting soggy and the Crunchberries are beginning to bloat."

"Oh, I'm sorry," I said. "I didn't know you were eating dinner."

"Nah, it's just a snack," she said. "For dinner, I'm having chocolate. At thirty-three, you can still do that."

"Yeah, you can," I agreed. "In fact, I spy with my big eye another can of spray cheese in the cupboard."

Walk All Over You

The flight attendant, his blue-vested chest puffed out like a rooster's, knelt beside the lady sitting next to me.

"I know you must hear this often," he gushed in a whisper loud enough for me to hear, "but I am your *biggest* fan! I know every word of every song you've ever sung, and I've seen all of your films."

The lady sitting next to me turned and smiled widely at the attendant literally kneeling below her, and nodded in a slow, almost queenly gesture.

"Thank you," she said quietly.

"It's such an *honor*—an absolute privilege—to have you aboard," the attendant continued, throwing an open hand onto his chest so hard it hit with a thud. "I cannot tell you. I am so honored. I—am—so—honored!"

The lady sitting next to me, still bearing the wide, expensive-lipstick-encrusted grin, closed her eyes softly, gave a nod duplicating her first, and parted her lips slightly, only to give another quiet "Thank you."

As soon as the attendant scurried away, the woman who had checked my boarding pass before I got on this plane suddenly appeared and leaned over to whisper closely into my neighbor's ear.

"I must thoroughly apologize for what happened back at the gate," I heard her say. "I'm so sorry it was such . . . an inconvenience. The security searches are random, and there was no way of knowing it was . . . well, *you!* Please accept my apology on behalf on the crew and the airline."

Again, the lady sitting next to me, the smile still frozen on her face, nodded and bequeathed a "Thank you" to the woman.

"I am your *biggest* fan," the boarding-pass lady then relented. "I just *love you!* I used to try to dance just like you."

The lady sitting next to me nodded and smiled. "Thank you," she said again quietly.

Wow, what a show, I thought to myself. Finally, my frequent-flier miles have paid off and the lucky upgrade that launched me into first class has landed me right next to a movie star. I had heard rumors that although my accumulation of frequent-flier miles wasn't going to get me to Europe, if I played my cards right, it would land me in a big leather seat in first class for absolutely nothing. It worked like this: If there was a seat that a rich person didn't spend a ridiculous amount on just so that they could get free drinks and eat fancier peanuts, all I had to do was flash my frequent-flier card and I was upgraded to sit among the chosen people.

Right.

For almost two years, I had been flashing that card as soon as I checked in, but it was always met with a disdainful look that seemed to say, "You . . . *silly peasant person!* How dare you think your kind could slip into the elite section! Back to the cattle car with you! Why, you're just lucky we even let you people *sit down!*"

But I wasn't about to give up on my dream. I'll hunt something down for the rest of my life if there's a chance I can get it for free or a relatively good discount. My little corn-teeth have elongated to the length of Julia Roberts's horse choppers because I can't seem to find time to floss and my gums are receding, but if I can get $3.00 off a bag of Kitty Litter with the right coupon, I'll pursue it harder than I did a husband.

But finally, it happened, despite the fact that I wasn't the only person who had trouble believing it.

"You're in first class?" the ticket lady, who was now kneeling like a subject in front of the lady next to me, had asked quietly when I tried to get on the plane.

"Oh yes," I answered as I handed her my first-class boarding pass. "I'm eccentric. I like to dress like a poor person. A DuPont lived in a bird's nest for years and years and then he started killing wrestlers! Rich people are all very odd. My money has caused me to snap and start wearing overalls. In fact, I'm building a nest myself. Would you mind if I took that quarter-size ball of lint from your sweater and added it to my new home? It would look perfect in the kitchen."

And then, moments after I took my seat, clearly more consumed with the fact that I was in first class and not who was in first class with me, I was not only sitting next to a rich person, but it was a famous rich person to boot and the airline people were freaking out.

Now I, naturally, being the polite, private, live-and-let-celebrities-live sort of person that I am, did not turn my head and stare at the mysterious famous person next to me. I did not. Even though the temptation to do so was scratching away at me from the inside like a rat would claw at trash, even though the desire was filling my insides up like a balloon ready to burst with helium, even though it was the one thing that I wanted to do more desperately than anything I've ever wanted to do in my life aside from vomiting the moment my husband chewed on a chitlin, I kept my composure and stared straight ahead.

And that's exactly what I did, for an *entire three seconds*.

And then I had to turn and look at her. What choice did I have? Here was an authentic (or at least a relatively high percentage of authenticity, most likely within the seventy-fifth to eightieth percentile) famous person sitting next to me. How could I not look? How could I not gawk? It was nearly inhuman not to turn my head and pick apart her features until I recognized her or was fairly confident that I could find a flaw that I could mock her secretly with.

Who could it be, I wondered as I turned my head to ogle her. Who could it be? She was a singer, an actress, and a dancer. Who, who, *who*?

Oh my God, my mind raced, maybe it is, Liza Minnelli, I hoped. Liza! Mizzzz Liza! Oh! Oh! Oh! Please let her be drunk, God, please let her be drunk and on goofballs! Life is a cabaret, old chum, it certainly is, it *certainly* is, although out of the corner of my eye, I could tell that my next-door neighbor celebrity's hair was too long and blondish to be Liza. Suddenly, I gasped. Maybe it's Ann-Margret, maybe it's Ann-Margret and we could talk about Elvis! Or Charo!! Maybe it's Charo! Oh, what are the chances? Oh, God, please let it be Charo, I begged, *please* let it be Charo and not a Landers sister!! Coochie-coochie, God! Please, coochie-coochie!! She's a spitfire! She's a pistol! We could sing the whole way to L.A.!

Coochie-coochie!!!

Oh shit, I thought, as a grisly vision popped into my head. What if it's . . . Carrot Top?

But I saw as soon as I finished my head turning and took in a good long gape, that it wasn't Charo, it wasn't Ann-Margret, it wasn't Liza, and to my relief, not the human Dreamsicle Carrot Top, because that would have been simply enough for me to flee right back to coach.

The truth is, I didn't know who the hell it was. I didn't have the slightest of ideas.

Oh well, I sighed to myself, she probably makes Lifetime movies or hocks something like "Face-Lift/Ass-Tuck in a Jar" on QVC. Now, if my mother was here, she'd probably know exactly who this lady was and might possibly start harping about how the Face-Lift in a Jar was more like "You Mean 'Lift My Hopes and then Kick Me in the Face' You Lying Son of a Bitch Jar" and she would be very appreciative if the lady would give her a refund by the time they touched down in Los Angeles, because people go to hell for things like that, you know. A check would be just fine.

But the lady next to me had to be rich, I knew that, because she was shopping for a house in the L.A. *Times* real estate section, and my detective's eyes saw that she had circled some chunks of land that held a pretty hefty price tag. I guess that's what kind of reward life hands you after you sell truckloads of shitty face cream to ladies who looked like they have potstickers under their eyes.

As we were taking off, I thought of a brilliant idea: Since I was in the first row, the flight attendant in the vest was strapped into his seat, facing me. When we hit a slight bump, he broke his stalker-like gaze at my neighbor, and I was able to catch his attention.

"Who is that?" I mouthed, nodding my head in the famous lady's direction.

The flight attendant scoffed and looked offended. "NANCY SINATRA," he mouthed disgustedly at me and then shook his head.

WHOA.

WHOA! Nancy Sinatra? *Nancy Sinatra!* "These Boots Are Made for Walkin' " Nancy Sinatra?

Wow, I said inside my head, spying on her seems so much more interesting now! Okay, it's no coochie-coochie, but she *was* the Chairman's daughter and that counted for a whole lot, especially in my family.

If you even begin to mention the name "Frank" or blithely make the "f" sound in front of my Nana, she will not hesitate to tell you what undoubtedly is the biggest story of her life:

"When Pop Pop and I were living in New York before the war, he took me to the Brooklyn Paramount one night to see Tommy Dorsey. During the show, he announced that somebody new was going to sing, and out popped this skinny fellow. What a beautiful voice! We were crazy about him! On the way out, I looked at the sign outside the Paramount and I saw the name Frank Sinatra. I said to Pop Pop. 'Hey, he's Italian! Let's remember his name, he was such a good singer!' "

Nana will tell anyone this story with unbridled enthusiasm and ultimate joy. Sadly, the remainder of her life experiences were unparalleled to seeing Frank Sinatra sing for the first time when he was a nobody, especially *after* he became FRANK SINATRA, His Royal Highness of the Italian Americans. In our world, he had more power than the Pope. So nothing, not even the birth of my mother ("What's the big deal?" Nana is known to have said. "The doctor gave me a shot and I went to sleep, then I woke up and had a baby. No biggie, believe me! I've worked harder peeling potatoes!") or the day Pop Pop returned from the war (he, by the way, after spending three years on various European fronts, living in mud, eating out of cans, and writing letters dutifully every day, came home to an empty house due to the fact that Nana apparently got hungry while she was waiting for his homecoming and went out to get a bite to eat), could compare to the beacon of a skinny, unknown Frank Sinatra.

Nothing.

And now, sitting next to me, sitting approximately seven inches away by my estimation—granted, I am slightly lackluster in the spatial relations department, so it may have been as much as a foot—was Nancy Sinatra, the closest thing left of the Chairman on this earth.

I mean, our elbows were almost touching. I was close enough to pass her a virus. In fact, I was closer to Nancy than Nana ever was to Frank.

And that's when I realized I had a problem.

There I was sitting next to Nancy Sinatra, and I already couldn't wait to tell everybody, especially Nana. And there was no way that I could tell my Nana what had just happened without her looking me in the face and asking, "What did she say when you told her that Pop and I saw Frank Sinatra at the Paramount before he was famous? And what did she say when you told her that I looked for his name? And that I remembered his name? What did she say? What did she say?"

It was then that I understood that I was going to have to break down and become one of *them*.

I was going to have to become a fan.

The realization was ugly, at best. Nancy Sinatra was not my first celebrity encounter, however. On the contrary; I am a seasoned celebrity encounterer. When I worked at Pizza D'Amore in high school, I served three slices of pepperoni to Sugar Ray Leonard and kept it cool by only asking him three times how he liked it, telling him that I put the pepperoni on those slices *personally*, if he hadn't noticed, in the shape of an S, an R, and an L. I bumped into Al Roker on Sixth Avenue in New York and completely stopped myself from saying an automatic "Hi," although a somewhat long "Haaaaaa———" escaped before I realized what I was doing, which would account for the look of horror on Al's face as he jumped into the street like the Lucky Charms elf and was nearly flattened by a FedEx truck as he tried to flee from me. I once mistook Maria Shriver for a girl I went to high school with, but I don't really consider yelling "Still snotty after all of these years, huh?" at her a freakout, since I believed her to be someone altogether different.

The only time I have really ever freaked out when spotting a celebrity was when I did indeed see Carrot Top and the volcano of protruding cheekbones and alleged "eyebrow realignment" that he has become, looking not only permanently startled but desperately malnourished as well. And a little like a lady, as long as we're being honest. Frankly, I always figured that it was against all odds that you would ever see the big orange menace in daylight, given that I believed Satan kept that little imp in a box and only let him out on special occasions or religious holidays to scramble about the world to instigate mayhem and breed hate among humans. But then again, that's pretty much what he was doing when I saw him hangin' with his homies in Santa Monica, his eyebrows lifted to his hairline and the flames of hell that double for his hair flying all over the place. He glanced in my direction and I fully believe was responsible for the Mr. Twisty pretzel dropping from my hands onto the dirty sidewalk, where a filthy homeless man wearing nothing but a loincloth beat me to the punch and had himself a nice Mr. Twisty supper.

But Miss Nancy Sinatra was no such demon, even though I was very hesitant to start up a conversation. In fact, my mouth dried up and my hands started to sweat and I noticed that I was trembling.

I was afraid. Now, I'm not exactly sure what I was afraid of—I mean, she seemed nice and cordial and cheery to everyone else. But I spent the next hour going back and forth—should I say something, should I not say something—and several times I cleared my throat to begin telling Nancy Sinatra Nana's tale, but then I would chicken out at the last moment.

I just didn't want to be one of those people, the kind of person who tells an insignificant story to someone they think gives a shit when they couldn't care less, particularly a famous person. I'm sure that my Nana's story wasn't going to be the first time she heard someone tell her about seeing her father singing when he was a skinny little kid; it probably wouldn't even rank in the first thousand times she'd heard it. In fact, it most likely happened to her on a regular basis, maybe even hourly. Why would she care? Why would Nancy Sinatra give a shit?

And all of a sudden, I realized that I didn't really need to be concerned with that. I didn't really need to care if I was boring Nancy Sinatra with an age-old story. Because I wasn't telling the story for me, and I wasn't telling the story for her. I was telling it for Nana. I was telling it for the pride Nana carried with her for sixty years, and how seeing Frank Sinatra was one of the most significant moments in her life.

I was going to tell Nancy because Nana never got to tell Frank.

And once I understood that, I cleared my throat and said to Nancy Sinatra, "Ms. Sinatra, I'm sorry to interrupt you," for which she must have taken me at my word, because she just kept reading the L.A. *Times* real estate section. So I cleared my throat again and said much, much louder, "MS. SINATRA, I'M SORRY TO IN-TERRUPT YOU," after which Nancy Sinatra turned and looked at me.

"I'm sorry, I know you're busy, but this will only take a minute," I said quickly as she stared at me. "Before the war, my grandparents, Nana and Pop Pop, saw your father singing with Tommy Dorsey at the Brooklyn Paramount, and after the show, my Nana made it a point to look at the marquee and catch his name. And she said to my Pop Pop, 'Nick, we have to remember that Frank Sinatra kid because he's Italian and has a beautiful voice.' She loves that story, and she loved your father."

"Thank you," Nancy Sinatra replied with a quick smile before returning to the newspaper.

Honestly, I was surprised. That's it? That's all I got for the last hour of torture I had been through? You gotta be kidding, Nancy Sinatra, give me more than that! I screamed in my head. Maybe I hadn't moved her enough, I decided. Maybe she had heard the story far too often.

I cleared my throat again.

"AND THEN," I said as I tapped her on the shoulder this time and she turned to look at me again, "and then at my wedding, my Pop Pop, the same one who had seen your father sing, was sick with cancer and had to come in a wheelchair. He couldn't walk very well by that point, and he had a blanket on his lap because he was cold. I was a little concerned, because he was really looking forward to our special dance later. You know, once my Pop Pop set his mind to something, he didn't stop until it was done, and he loved to dance to Frank Sinatra records. He was a great dancer. But for the first time, I wasn't sure if he could pull it off, he wasn't looking too good. Then, when the time came, and the first notes of Pop's favorite song—your father singing 'Fly Me to the Moon' (oh, do I owe you royalties for that?)—were played, my Pop Pop threw that blanket to the ground and started strutting around like a *Solid Gold* dancer, even I couldn't keep up with him. Some people started crying, throwing up their hands and saying it was a miracle, that he was not only walking, he was dancing. But I think it was that song. He loved that song and the way your father sang it. We had such a good time out there, he danced and we were laughing, and laughing, and laughing. I really loved my Pop. We had a great time. And as it turned out, that was the last time Pop Pop ever got to dance. We . . . well, we lost him a couple of weeks after that. But at least that last dance was to his favorite song, he really . . . he really loved that song."

Now, by this point, even I, the girl with the meanest, coldest little black heart in all of the world, had a lump in her throat, and I had to turn my head away quickly, because I was in great danger of Publicly Expressing a Private Emotion. Which is not cool AT ALL. When I looked back a moment later, Nancy Sinatra was looking at me. And then, suddenly, she turned her head and went right back to her newspaper without saying a word.

Nancy Sinatra did not give a shit.

I wasn't even sure if I cared. I don't think I did. I mean, I had said what I needed to say, and that was that. It was all I needed to go back to Nana and tell her that I had told Nancy Sinatra her story. Nothing else really mattered. And if Nancy couldn't give forty seconds of her time to hear a story about people who really loved her father, then I didn't give a shit, either.

I was at the baggage claim when I saw her again, flanked by her personal assistant and her driver. My suitcase came out immediately, and as I pulled it off the carrier, I turned around and I was face-to-face with her. And that's when I knew that I was lying, because it turns out that I did give a shit. I did. My grandparents spent decades idolizing Frank Sinatra, watching his movies, buying every record, making sure to watch every single television special, tuning into radio stations that played his music, going back to the Brooklyn Paramount repeatedly to see their favorite new singer. I *totally* gave a shit.

And this was my last chance to say it.

"I'm really sorry that I wasted your time with my dumb little stories," I said to Nancy Sinatra. "But your dad was really important to my family, and I thought you should know. I thought you might like to hear that."

She looked startled. She looked very surprised.

"Oh," she said slowly, and she brought her hand up to her face. "No, no, no, they were lovely. Lovely stories. I just—my daughter is getting married in a few weeks, and we're playing that same song at her wedding, for my father. And your story . . . it just reminded me of that. It's . . . *hard*, you know?"

I nodded. I did know. And I also knew, just then, that Nancy Sinatra gave a shit.

"I loved hearing those stories," she said with a very gentle smile. "Thank you."

I nodded and I smiled back.

"Thank you," I said.

Acknowledgments

In lieu of taking everyone out to dinner, I'd like to extend some special thanks. Stop the whining, a free dinner will be forgotten and gone in approximately twelve hours, while your name in print will last a lifetime, or at least for the time it takes for this book to wind up in the outlet stores, when you cheap bastards will finally buy it because you never got the free copy I promised you.

Thanks:

To Jenny Bent, without whom I'd still have a shitty job. A million thanks for a million things—for being the first one in a really long time to believe in me, for the counseling, for listening to me, for letting me talk, for telling me to shut up, and for the biggest prune I will never forget. Oh my God, that was a joke!

To Bruce Tracy, for his patience, direction, support, and friendship, and for letting me keep my voice. Unfortunately, I've had editors who are as bad as he is good, and thus, I know enough to appreciate how lucky I am. And I know it.

To my family, for not disowning me after I wiped the shame well dry, for pretending they thought the first book was good, and for not vaporizing my advance by calling in all of my loans. That would have sucked.

Thanks to my ball and chain, who usually just sits and shakes his head. I'm sorry you married a big ole bag of trouble like me, but God gave me big boobs to make up for it. You are the best in the world right now, you know.

To my dad, who foolishly passed out my first book to his friends and colleagues without reading it first, for assaulting warehouse shoppers with it in Costco and harassing them until they bought it, and for teaching me: 1) never buy anything in a dented box; 2) anyone who doesn't agree with you is an idiot; and 3) anyone who ever fired me was an asshole and dumber than dog shit. Thanks, Dad, and thanks for supporting me when I was jobless and drumming up material for the book, or in other words, "lazy." But sorry, I still, apparently, cannot hang on to a job in any capacity.

To my mom, who now finally understands that her life is nothing now but a source of material, for being a really good sport, and for keeping her shoe on and not smacking me every time she sees me. You rock, Mom. No, Mom, I didn't mean it in a dirty way.

To Nick and David, thanks for the material that you have yet to provide, and don't worry about it, I'll do for you what Grandma did after she ruined me and pay for your psychotherapy. Fair and square. You are both the best little boys ever and I love you so much. And a very special thanks to your mom for getting Aunt Laurie off of the reproductive hook, so to speak.

To Nana, who makes me laugh, tells me crazy stories, and always surprises me. I have the best Nana ever.

To the Idiot Girls, Jamie, Nikki, Sara, Kate, Sandra, and Krysti, and the Idiot Guy, Jeff—sorry for all the embarrassment I caused you after the last book, but HEY, you got your name in the liner notes and didn't even have to diddle a guy in the band for it, so STOP COMPLAINING! I am lucky to have you as friends, and even luckier that we're still friends.

To David Dunton, for being the best friend I only met once, for helping me through some pretty rough spots, for dorking out with me, and for Prime Burger. Forever appreciated, truly.

To Pamela Cannon, for striking the match, and for being one of the coolest chicks I could have ever hoped to know.

To Meg Halverson, Bill Hummel, Theresa Cano, Kathy Murillo, Coni Bourin, Laura K. Smith, Alexa Cassanos, Katie Zug, Sessalee Hensley, Jules Herbert, Donna Passanante, Nina Graybill, Annie Klein, Lisa Dicker, Brent Babb, Curtis Grippe, Brian Griffith, Steve Larson, Patrick Sedillo, Charlie Levy, Jon Kinyon, Jamal Ruhe, Dave Purcell, Monica Reid, Craig Browning, Duane Neff, Amy Silverman, Sonda Andersson-Pappan, Beth Kawasaki, Eric Searleman, Charlie Pabst, Bill Homuth, Sharon Hise, the Public Library Association, the Arizona Library Association, the ladies at the B&N in Fairfax, Ms. Nancy Sinatra, and, of course, bookstores little and big for your help, kindness, support, or for not calling security on me.

And, most important, to Idiot Girls all over the world and everyone who read the last book, wrote a letter, dropped me an e-mail, passed the book on to a friend, confessed that they belonged in the club, stopped by to say hi, or came to a reading: THANK YOU. THANK YOU THANK YOU THANK YOU. The best part is meeting you, laughing with you, and knowing that I'm not the only one. You know what I mean.

You rule.

love, laurie n.

ABOUT THE AUTHOR

LAURIE NOTARO has never written for Rolling Stone, Esquire, Harper's, The New Yorker, Truckin', Lowrider, Coin World, Knives Illustrated, Whispers from Heaven, Dog Fancy, American Logger, Farm Show, Supermodels Unlimited, or McSweeney's. She lives, and will probably die, in Phoenix, Arizona. Miraculously, this is her second book.

Here she is at her wedding reception, mere minutes after getting married and apparently returning from a satisfying trip to the meatball pyramid. As her lucky new spouse closes the deal by signing the marriage license, his new bride is not only taking that opportunity to dig a meatball particle out of her teeth with her tongue, but has also completely abandoned the effort of sucking her stomach in, never to return.